D1159944

PUC

Gray Dog
of
Norway

NINA P. ROSS

ILLUSTRATED BY JEAN HOLMGREN

Copyright © 1995 The Best of Times, Inc.

All rights reserved. No part of this work may be reproduced or copied in any form or by any means, except for brief excerpts in conjunction with book reviews, without prior written permission from the publisher.

Printed on acid-free paper
Manufactured in the United States of America

Library of Congress Cataloging-in-Publication Data

Ross, Nina P., 1931–
    PUC, Gray Dog of Norway/Nina P. Ross: illustrations
by Jean Holmgren.
        p. cm.
    Includes bibliographical references.
    ISBN 1-886049-04-1
    1.

Book design and layout by
    Lori Leath-Smith

THE BEST OF TIMES, INC.

P.O. Box 1360
Pelham, Alabama 35124

dedicated to

our many friends in Norway

TABLE OF CONTENTS

PROLOGUE

NORWAY IS A MYTHICAL LAND OF LEGEND,
still emerging from its cocoon of icy debris, scooped for
centuries from the top of the world. It can be a winter wonderland where the wicked ice giants of the North play havoc
with anything that gets in their way. Simultaneously the
midnight sun can clothe Norway in eerie mystique—a ro-
mantic aura for the idyllic, a depressant for the dispirited.
And with the coming of spring, as it has since the beginning
of time, the icy water of winter drains from the snowcapped
mountains into the fingerlike fjords below. And then it
becomes a summer playground where those same mountains
are covered with blue berries and red berries, white daisies
and cloudberries, a palette of paint to which any artist would
succumb. And the legends of its past are slowly exposed.

There was a time toward the end of the Ice Age when
man and animals first arrived on the coast of Norway by
crossing the frozen sea from the European mainland. They
began their voyage in southern Norway, the first mass of
land to emerge from the great glacier that covered all of
Scandinavia for thousands of years. As the ice receded and
forests began to cover the mountains, great herds of reindeer
followed the thick foliage toward the ice cap of the interior.
The herds were stalked every step of the way by small bands
of hunters.

The hunters and gatherers, as they are referred to in the study of civilization, continued their procession through the ages—Stone, Bronze, Iron, and Viking. They chronicled for posterity their descent through the centuries by polluting the environment with a trail of refuse for archaeologists to play with and graffiti on the rocks at which tourists continue to marvel. A few thousand Samelats cling to the traditions of their forefathers within the bounds of the barren polar region of Norway and Russia, their reliance still on the reindeer for survival.

The people of Norway, proud of their heritage, don their national costumes to celebrate national days, holidays, or just to celebrate—the tall, blond, fair-skinned people of Nordic descent; the shorter, fair-skinned Sami people of unknown descent; the third world immigrants who claim Norway as home.

Norway, like many countries of the world, has a national anthem, a national flag, a national coat of arms, and numerous other national symbols that are mentioned at one time or another in a fact book, encyclopedia, or textbook. Norwegians, like citizens of many other countries, are often oblivious of some of their national symbols. For instance, one such symbol was commemorated on an official postage stamp of Norway on February 16, 1983. That same symbol was adopted by the Norsk Kennel Klub as its logo in 1898. But not many Norwegians are aware of the fact that the gray elkhound—the symbol on the postage stamp and the logo of the kennel club—is the national dog of Norway. Chances are very likely that many Norwegians have never even seen a gray elkhound and in many instances would not know it if they happened to sit by one on the bus or train. That is a definite possibility because it is not at all unusual for dogs to accompany their owners on public transportation, in stores, and in a few restaurants in Norway.

Norwegians are outdoor people. They take to skis at a very early age. They do not rely on cars and superhighways to the extent that people do in countries farther from the Arctic. Their ability to navigate during their harsh arctic winters has helped them to become some of the most avid sportsmen in the world. In fact, Norway is regarded as the birthplace of the modern sport of skiing. The Norwegian skiers reaffirmed this by winning gold medals at all but one Winter Olympics beginning with the first Olympics in Chamonix, France, in 1924, to the latest in Lillehammer in 1994. Norway hosted the sixth Winter Olympics in Oslo in 1952 and had entries in 22 events.

Hunting is an outdoor sport of a different kind, although it often includes skiing. During the tough years in Norway's history, hunting was necessary for survival. For centuries, the men supplied their families with wild game to keep them from starving to death. For centuries, the men have been accompanied on the hunt by a dog from the spitz family—the gray elkhound. There are black elkhounds, white elkhounds, and yellow elkhounds. The yellow elkhounds are actually buhunds that have much the same conformation as black elkhounds. The gray elkhound, however, is a distinct breed, the national dog of Norway. It is usually referred to as the Norwegian Elkhound in countries other than in Scandinavia.

The gray elkhound is a highly intelligent dog that hunts by scent as well as by sight. It is well equipped with a repellent double coat to enable it to endure freezing weather and precipitation. Perhaps its aristocratic appearance and aloofness set it apart from the other elkhound breeds, for they are all hunters by nature.

When an elkhound trails a moose and keeps it at a stand until the hunter makes the kill, the elkhound is credited with the moose. "My Bella has six moose already this year," boasts a proud hunter. A hunter may spend days at a time on a hunt with his dog as his only companion. During that time of camaraderie, a hunter and his dog speak the same language, share thoughts, and live and die for one another. Perhaps the stories that are told over and over again by hunters have immortalized the gray elkhound or, for the skeptic, at least made the dog's antics plausible.

The story of Puc is centered around Osh, a typical hunter, like his father before him. He and his friends train their dogs in ample time before the hunting season opens in September. Osh, Arne, and Liv, like all hunters, must be physically fit to traipse the rocky terrain and endure the often inclement weather. Leidi, a typical hunting elkhound, has the added responsibility to procreate. The focus of the story centers on Puc, the star of Leidi's last litter. As the story of Osh and Puc unravels, like the thawing ice of the glaciers, perhaps it will expose the versatility of the gray elkhound and reiterate the bonding of man and dog, as one tries to outwit the other.

First of All

THE FURRY FIGURE WAS BARELY PERCEPTIBLE in the Nordic twilight. The shimmery effervescence of the snowfields caused luminous shadows to lurk where there were no shadow makers, only figments. It had taken weeks for the weary animal to make its way this far. The shadows that at one point provided a diversion in the long journey no longer posed a threat. There was not even an effort by the animal to camouflage the deep telltale path it made in the snow by zigzagging or backtracking as it knew instinctively that it should. Instead, it dragged its heavy body around the simple wooden building that loomed in its pathway.

The structure was the first hint of human habitation that the dog encountered in her descent from the mountain into this remote arctic village. The closed doors of the building offered no haven for the aching body that was searching for a place to lie down. There was nothing for her

1

to do but hobble on to search the next building that loomed in the half-light. The building of hand hewn logs was a school, still strong with the smell of the Sami boys and girls who spent the better part of a darkened day within its four walls. It stood empty but, like the building before it, there was no way into the safety of its inner sanctum.

The mysterious light of the midnight sun had dimmed months earlier so that the fjords and mountains were in darkness. Most of the days were stormy and the nights, though cold and dark, were at least peaceful.

Just as the lost dog felt the first pang of the birthing process, she spotted a pulka that was parked near the front door of a simple wooden house on the outskirts of the village. The pulka still held the crude reindeer skin cover that was used for protection against the blustery wind. The cover was spread over the rough wooden frame, causing it to look much like the animal from which it was taken. Earlier that day the pulka, pulled by reindeer, had traveled over the deep snow of the arctic winter to bring in a supply of wood. Now it sat empty, a veritable manger in all its crudity. Leidi thrust her heaving body into the sled and began the inevitable ritual of whelping.

Lapland extends across northern Norway, Sweden, Finland, and the Kola Peninsula of Russia. Most of it is inside the Arctic Circle. The western portion is pitted with fjords, deep valleys, glaciers, and mountains. The low plateau of the eastern portion, where marshes and lakes dominate the landscape, is just as barren. However, reindeer, wolves, bears, and sea and land fowl inhabit the southern portion where vegetation is sparse except in the

densely forested area. It was through this area that Leidi had
chosen—as the crow flies—to return home.

Lapps, a Ural-Altaic people, have no country of their
own. They are citizens of the country in which they maintain their permanent villages. They are better known as
Sami or Samelats. Their numbers have dwindled throughout
the years until only about 34,000 of them are left, of which
20,000 reside in Norway. Although fewer than one-third
of the Sami people are nomadic, others live in permanent
settlements on the coast, near fjords, and in villages at the
heads of valleys where there are well-stocked lakes. Only a
few of them continue to go through life herding reindeer for
food and clothing, and supplementing their needs by hunting
and fishing. More and more of them find work in the iron
mines or lumber and pulp mills. Even as they begin to assert
their rights to their heritage, many of them live in relative
isolation in small villages. It was into one of these villages
that the staggering dog found refuge.

Leidi is a hunting dog used to track moose. The meat of
the moose is a staple food for many Norwegian families.
Therefore, a good hunting dog is a valuable asset and is
treated as respected property because of its contribution to the
welfare of its owners. Leidi has many moose to her credit
and has won the respect and admiration of many hunters in
the area. She is owned by a Norwegian family that lives
near Storskog outside the town of Kirkenes.

Kirkenes is a sizable town in the extreme northeastern
corner of Norway near the borders of Finland and Russia. It
serves as the hub of activity in the area with its schools,
hospital, shopping, air transportation, and shipping. It

accommodates many of the inhabitants of Storskog, a small place to the east, when they are in need of materials and services that are not available in Storskog. Still farther east is a forest, a favorite area for moose hunters, especially Osh.

As was usual for the opening of the hunting season which affords a golden opportunity to fill the larder for the long, hard winter, Leidi set out on a hunting trip with Osh, who was her owner, and his two friends, Arne and Liv. The hunt was to take place in one of the forests on the opposite side of the mountain from the Sami village. The men hunted the area many times and were familiar with the treacherous terrain. They knew also that it was a stomping ground for hordes of moose.

The men met at Osh's farmhouse early one frosty morning. Experience had taught them to take enough food and survival supplies in the event a winter storm forced them to spend the night. It was not unusual for the sky to turn gray, and, as the old folks used to say, for the wicked ice giants to shake their featherbeds—dyne—so hard that the eiderdown covered the mountains.

When the ample supplies were loaded into the four-wheel drive jeeps, the happy party, including Leidi, started out. They circled the mountain over bumpy pathways and through mountain passes. They finally emerged on the tract of forest to which their hunting party was assigned by the hunting commission for the season. It was a long drive but hiking up and over the mountain—although closer—was next to impossible, especially with the weight of all the gear necessary for the hunt.

Since they were quite a distance from home, the men planned to spend several nights in the camp. They would need more in the way of equipment and supplies than hunters who were out for a long day would need. Like campers, they brought along their primus, the petrol fire that would boil coffee, water, and anything else the men might want to heat. The tents and sleeping bags that they packed would be a welcome luxury after a cold day of following a big moose up and down the steep mountain. It took both jeeps, piled high, to transport all their paraphernalia.

At last the party arrived at the camp. It was nothing more than a small clearing where the men could pitch their tents and stow their supplies while they were on the trail with the dog. A few years ago the men had nailed a makeshift table and bench between two trees. The rough table served as a place to load and unload. It also provided a step up for them when they needed to lasso a high branch in the tree to suspend a moose carcass if they were staying for a few days—and hunting was good. The men unloaded the vehicles and secured their staples, knowing full well that a marauding bear could and would demolish the camp for as little as a candy bar.

Leidi would be hunting off lead. Osh made last-minute assignments of responsibilities to the men, designating which man would respond to the signals given by the dog while she was stalking a moose. Arne and Liv would stop at a strategic location along the trail in case the moose changed its course.

Leidi would follow the moose's scent, possibly for hours before she was able to bring it to a stand. She would accomplish this by running in circles around the huge animal, all the while nipping at its legs and making a real pest of herself. Like all well-trained dogs, she knew when to bark and when to remain silent. At that point she would give a shrill continuous bark, a signal that it was time for a hunter to creep in for the kill. Any abrupt movement or crackling twig could set the moose in motion and the dog would have to start the stalking all over again. Each hunter was pledged to assume responsibility for his own actions to insure the well-being of his comrades as well as the safety of the dog.

It did not take long for the men to organize. Each hunter donned a backpack that contained emergency supplies. No hunter in his right mind would go out into the forest without a survival kit, a thermos of hot coffee or hot chocolate to drink, and jerky or cookies to nibble. The hunters' knives hung in leather sheaths around their waists, except for Osh, who wore his strapped to his leg. Last, but most importantly, they picked up their guns, and the hunt was on.

Leidi was a good hunter. It was not long after the men gave her the command to hunt that she found the scent of a moose. With her head held high to catch the scent as it lifted from the ground, she forgot everything but the moose that was somewhere farther along the trail. The hunters stayed well back, knowing that Leidi would signal them when she had the moose in position. She followed what appeared to be a big bull moose for several hours. The cow and calf had vanished into the forest after several kilometers and were no

longer visible. Only the heavy hoofprints of the bull continued to appear. The moose went up a steep grade, doubled
back, and descended into a thick grove of trees. It jumped a
noisy stream and headed up again. Leidi followed noise-
lessly. She caught a whiff of the big animal's scent and had
to wade an icy stream. Once on the other side, she gave a
vigorous shake to rid her water-repellent coat of water and
continued the hunt.

A herd of reindeer ambled in a nearby clearing. They
knew that the gray dog was not a threat to them. Although
Leidi was aware of their presence, she knew to ignore them
as well as the airborne scents of other animals. Her target
was the moose up ahead and the moose knew it. At last
Leidi was close enough to start the circling, nipping, and
incessant barking that would hold the big animal's attention
while Osh and the other hunters got close enough for a shot.

Osh was cutting through the dense grove of trees rather
than going around it. He knew from past experience that
Leidi was getting close to stalling the moose and he wanted
to be in a good position to take careful aim. If he should
miss his mark and wound the moose, it would mean wasted
time. Leidi would have to track the wounded animal so that
it could be destroyed. Hunters are required by law to have
with them on the hunt a dog that can track wounded animals. Osh was an expert marksman and usually bagged his
target with one clean shot, although he occasionally missed
completely. He could not bear the thought of wounding a
moose and causing it to suffer until it was found and relieved
of pain.

Osh came out of the grove and stepped over a fallen tree just as he heard Leidi's first shrill bark. In startled anticipation, he swung his other leg over the log. Much to his dismay, his trouser leg caught on the stump of a branch that was protruding from the downed tree. In an effort to regain his balance, Osh brought his other foot down, not knowing that a moss-covered rock was hidden by the snow in front of him. He stumbled and plunged headfirst down a steep embankment. His efforts to grab at saplings that were bent over by an early snow were in vain, and he continued head-over-heels down the incline.

Arne and Liv also heard Leidi's bark, followed quickly by Osh's yell as he tripped. There was no time now for them to creep in for the kill. Instead, they made their way toward the sound of Osh's yell. They spotted his motionless body, draped around the base of a tree about halfway down the slope. Leidi's bark signaling that she had the moose at a stand sent an echo reverberating through the forest. Unknown to Leidi, her efforts were of no avail. Arne and Liv did not even think to call her off the hunt.

Osh needed them and he needed them right now. From the way it looked from their vantage point, they would have to fashion a stretcher to bring him back up the embankment. They could cut some of the young birch saplings that were growing on the slope. The deep snow provided a good foothold each step of the way down, slowly but with no danger of slipping or falling. Osh was barely conscious when they reached him. Before moving him, the men cut two saplings of equal size to accommodate Osh's body length. They hacked the branches off the slender trunks and then found two pieces of equal size for the cross sections. They lashed the pieces together into a stretcher frame, using the straps from their backpacks. They made sure the frame would slide snugly inside the sleeping bag which Arne pulled from his own backpack.

Arne eased the stretcher under Osh as Liv eased Osh onto the sleeping bag. Osh groaned with every touch to his bruised body. The men covered him with Liv's sleeping bag and began the difficult task of carrying him back to camp. They circled the grove of trees instead of climbing back up to the spot where Osh had tumbled. The deep snow acted as a cushion for the stretcher and was actually a gentler ride for Osh when one man pulled the stretcher than it was when they both tried to carry it.

In an effort to get medical help sooner, Arne went ahead to get a jeep from camp. It proved to be a wise decision because, by the time the jeep plowed its way to Osh, the injured man was already in shock and in grave danger with as yet undetermined injuries. The men loaded him carefully into the jeep and sped back to town, disregarding any traffic laws that may have existed. They would come back for Leidi later.

Ordinarily Osh would not have brought Leidi because she had been bred to Grom just three weeks ago. Grom was the most sought after stud dog in all of Norway. But the moose had been elusive this winter and Leidi was one of the best hunting dogs in this part of the country.

In the meantime, Leidi kept the moose at a standstill until the huge animal became too agitated at the pesky dog and bolted off in a trot into the dense forest. Leidi sensed

that something was wrong when her master did not respond
to her signal. She instinctively retreated to find the hunting
party, as all good hunting dogs do, even though she did not
hear the whistle Osh always used when she was beyond
voice range.

Leidi circled again and again, trying to find Osh. She
was confused by the sudden plunge of his scent down the
steep mountain. She found the tree where Osh had lain.
She found the backpacks, stripped of their straps and sleeping
bags. She followed the stretcher marks in the snow to the
place where the stretcher was loaded onto the jeep. She even
followed the jeep tracks back to camp but, when she got
there, the jeep was gone. She was alone. She had no choice
but to make her way back up and over the mountain. It was
a long way through the deep snow and the treacherous
terrain. But she knew she would get home eventually.

Winter raged on. The snow became deeper and deeper.
The scent of a moose lost its thrill. Leidi was hungry. She
began to concentrate more on finding food than she did on
finding her way home. More and more often she was too
tired and too weak to catch so much as a small rodent, even
when the rodent was spending the night under the same log.
She eventually came to the realization that she was hope-
lessly lost. Days turned into weeks and during those difficult
weeks, the puppies inside her warm body became heavy and
impatient. Her time of travail had come.

NINA P. ROSS

A Pulka Full of Puppies

N THE EARLY HISTORY OF NORWAY WHEN IT began its emergence from the icy shield that had held it captive since the beginning of time, herds of wild reindeer migrated into the southern portion of the country from Europe. They came over the land bridges and frozen sea. As the land emerged from the ice, lush forests sprouted. The herds followed the melting ice northward, thriving on the mossy flora that covered the newly exposed mountains.

The reindeer herds were followed by small groups of people who relied on the animals for survival. When the reindeer and people gradually reached the extent of their migratory journey, bounded in the still barren northlands by yet another sea, they maintained small herds of tame reindeer. The herds expanded as a result of orphaned calves that the people raised by hand and old cows and bulls that were content to graze along with the tamed youngsters.

The bands of people, now known as Samis, remained in

the arctic area and established permanent villages. Throughout the years the people, like the herds, have diminished in
number. A few persist in their nomadic ways. Others left
their peers to enter the larger Norwegian society, and a few
remain in their own villages.

The family living in the simple frame house on the
outskirts of the Sami village is typical of the other families in
the village. The inhabitants are all permanent residents of
the village, although the herdsmen take the reindeer to
summer pastures and remain with them until winter de-
scends on the mountains.

A few reindeer are kept at the village to supply milk
and, if necessary, to pull loads. The reindeer are also the
family's source of cheese and meat. In fact, the Sami were at
one time totally dependent on the reindeer for survival.
Reindeer skins were made into tents, blankets, moccasins,
leggings, and harnesses. The sinews were used for thread,
cord, and braided lassos. Even the bones and antlers were
made into tools and household utensils.

Today, as in centuries past, everyone in the Sami family
assumes the responsibility for doing certain chores.   Even
the animals that belong to the family must serve a purpose.
In addition to its other uses, the reindeer's job is to pull the
pulka that sits waiting near the door of the small house.
And that is what caught the boy's eye as he emerged from
the house to bring in wood for the morning fire, his first task
in helping his mother prepare the morning meal.

The house still held the darkness of the night. Lamps
were used only when absolutely necessary. And it was not
necessary for family members to have light to make their

way around inside the sparsely furnished house. The light
from the morning fire provided enough light for cooking,
eating, and getting ready for school.

"Pappa! Pappa!" As the boy's eyes became accustomed
to the outside light that was dancing from the diamond-
clustered snow, he spotted the pulka with its uninvited
passengers. Leidi's five newborn puppies were snuggled
against her like furry, black pompoms. Four of the puppies
were solid black. The fifth one had a small but perfectly
formed white star on its forefront. The puppies' stomachs
were full and they were warm against their dam's belly and
the hairy reindeer cover in the bottom of the pulka.

The sleepy bundles of fur were oblivious to the sudden
tautness of their mother's body as the boy approached. Leidi
gave a warning growl, but she did not move. Even though
she was completely exhausted from her trek over the mountain and from whelping a litter of puppies, Leidi was ready to
protect her brood in whatever way was necessary. The boy
was sensitive to her warning and stood back.

An older man opened the door to see what had
alarmed his young son. The man's blue eyes softened when
he saw the visitors that lay cuddled in the pulka. He immediately recognized Leidi as the gray dog used by the hunters
to track moose and not a gray wolf, the untamed and un-
wanted inhabitant of the sparsely wooded areas.

The man shuddered as he remembered the stories told
to him as a child by the parents of his grandparents—stories
of the utter devastation wreaked on all of the North country
by packs of wolves that killed every animal they could find
until the people themselves were starving from lack of food.

He remembered how, as a boy, he anticipated the old folks' telling of Gravind—or Wolf Night—that night long ago when the wolves were outwitted by a clever, great gray dog and subsequently killed by angry farmers.

He smiled to himself as he recognized the dog in the pulka as the great gray dog in his memory. The wolf remained as a threat to his reindeer herd, whereas the gray dogs of the hunters were trained to ignore the reindeer, cows, sheep, and horses of the farmers. He knew, too, the value that the hunters placed on their dogs and quickly surmised that this one, somehow, had become lost. In a small way, he could return the favor, pay back the debt owed to the gray dog by his ancestors. He would care for this dog until he could find her owners.

Leidi gave another warning growl when the two people moved toward her. She stood over her puppies, her legs wobbly from hunger and from giving birth. When the man spoke to his son to go on with his chores and let the dog alone, Leidi relaxed slightly. She knew from the tone of his voice that she was in no immediate danger.

The boy carried the wood inside the house so that his mother could rekindle the fire. He came back out of the house with a wooden bowl of reindeer milk. He set the bowl on the ground beside the house where Leidi could see it. Knowing that she would not move while he stood there, he returned to the stuffy kitchen. He and his sister watched the gray dog through the smoke-smudged window while his mother prepared the usual meal of mush, bread, cheese, and milk for the family.

Leidi ignored the bowl as long as she could, saliva

dripping from her quivering jowls. She eased out of the sled, disgusted with herself for being wobbly and stiff. With a look of trepidation at her squirming babies, she lurched for the milk and gulped it down before another crystal of ice had time to form around the edge of the bowl. Not even a cat with the keenest nose in all Lapland would have guessed that there was ever any milk in the bowl when Leidi finished.

Looking furtively at the pulka, Leidi took time to relieve herself and take a luxuriant roll in the snow to remove any lingering soil from whelping the puppies. It was the third time she had given birth, and, while it was painful at the time, her thoughts shifted from the pain to protecting the puppies in these strange surroundings. She hopped back into the pulka with much greater ease than she had the night before. Her grunting off-spring groped eagerly for another turn at Leidi's ample teats, kneading their legs into her stomach, snorting, sucking,

17

smacking, and gradually drifting off to sleep.

The routine of living was not going to change for the Sami family just because a stray dog had taken up residence in the pulka. Chores before school and chores after school took precedence over playing with puppies. The boy, however, knew that the new litter was his responsibility. He could hardly wait to pick the puppies up, especially the one that he noticed had a white star on its front. He threw a bone that was stripped clean of meat and a portion of mush that he salvaged from the morning repast toward the pulka when he and his sister left for school.

The children trudged through the slush on the well-worn path that wound past the cookie cutter houses of other Sami families in their village. Each house contributed one, two, three, or more children to the rowdy group as the youngsters made their way to the one-room schoolhouse in the center of the village. They would spend the better part of the day being taught to read, write, and do arithmetic in their Sami dialect, one of nine in the Sami language. Each dialect was so different that Sami people from other areas often experience difficulty in understanding one another and, sometimes, cannot understand each other at all.

The other children of the village soon heard about the new family in the pulka. Nothing in the world could keep them from coming to investigate after their school day is over. Stray dogs from the village knew, too. They came to investigate right away but, after receiving a snarling warning from Leidi, they kept a safe distance and pretended to ignore her.

Leidi immediately gobbled up the mush and hid the

bone under the reindeer cover in the pulka to keep the strays from taking it. A stern warning from the man inside the house sent the strays scampering on their way. The man had already decided what he was going to do about the gray dog and her litter of puppies.

In addition to the school, there was a church of hand hewn logs in the Sami village. The only thing to distinguish the church from the school was the shape of its roof and its double doors. The two buildings are the hub of social life for the Sami villagers. They hold fairs in the wintertime instead of summertime, partly because the reindeer herds are taken to coastal pastures for better grazing.

There are no local newspapers. Town meetings give the villagers an opportunity to catch up on the happenings in the village and to hear news that drifts in by way of travelers. The meetings provide forums where everyone has a right to voice an opinion. The Sami people, like the indigenous people in other parts of the world, take pride in their culture, preserving their past to ensure a future for their children—a unique link toward global diversity.

It was here at a town meeting that the man planned to lay claim to the gray dog. He felt that, for all practical purposes, the dog belonged to him. He would provide for it and let it care for its puppies in his pulka since that is where it had chosen to whelp. In the meantime, he would post a message where the hunters were likely to see it—above the table in their camp.

The hunters would be looking for their dog. Of that, he was sure. They need meat for their families just as he does. It seemed to the Sami, however, that the hunters'

system of survival worked better than his system. The
hunters always have an abundance of food in their camps.
Whenever he has an occasion to drive his herd past their
camps, he always stares in wonder at the provisions they
carry. They ride around in four-wheel drive vehicles . They
have a new contraption that looks like a pulka with a motor.
If he had one of those he could go to the mine to work and
not have to spend all his time with the herd. He would be
wealthy like the hunters.

The man just knew that when the hunters see the
sign he plans to nail to the trees in their camps that they will
come for the gray dog. When they come, he will tell them
what they owe him in return for caring for the dog and her
offspring. He will ask them for enough to compensate him
for the harsh winter he and his family have just endured.
That will even things up a little.

In the meantime, he will let the boy care for the gray
dog and her litter. The boy is too timid. He needs some
work and responsibility to toughen him up. Sami boys need
to grow up a little sooner than other boys. They need to
become men and take their places in the village. The young
people grow up and move away from the village all the
time—but not his son. His son will own the largest reindeer
herd. He will build a big house in the village. He will
become the leader of the village. The gray dog is his guaran-
tee that all this will come to pass.

In the Meantime

ARNE AND LIV WORKED QUICKLY. THEY EASED
Osh onto the sleeping bag that was stretched over the
birch branch frame. After they lashed Osh onto the makeshift stretcher so that he was immobile, they hoisted the
stretcher onto the back seat of the jeep. Osh's head protruded
on one side, his feet the other. Last of all they secured the
stretcher so that it dangled like a wind chime from the
overhead roll-frame of the jeep. In this manner, Osh would
not receive the full brunt of the bumpy ride back to the
highway. And bumpy it was.

The mountain appeared to be covered in a smooth,
velvety blanket of snow. Its empyreal appearance was a
mask of deception for Arne and Liv, however, in their effort
to spare Osh additional pain. The unseen boulders that lay
under the lavish layer of snow transformed the mountain
into an obstacle course. The minutes seemed like hours
before they reached the main road.

Once they were on the paved road they made the trip
back to town at breakneck speed. They went right to the first
aid station where a helicopter was waiting to take Osh to the
hospital in Kirkenes. Arne had radioed ahead to the station
to announce their impending arrival. Hospitals are located
strategically so that several towns are served by one hospital.
It is common practice to transfer patients by helicopter in
cases of emergency. Osh's case was an emergency.

The paramedics commended the two hunters on their
innovative stretcher and did not unbind Osh for the helicopter ride to the hospital. They gave him an injection to relieve
the pain and slipped an oxygen mask over his face as the
helicopter lifted off. Arne and Liv were relieved that Osh
was on his way to the hospital where he would receive
expert care. Now they had to attend to some unfinished
business. First, they called Osh's family and told them about
the accident. His wife and son were extremely upset, but
they were thankful that it was not an accidental shooting
incident. Osh, who was always careful and used every
precaution when he had a gun, would never forgive himself
if he had been the cause of an accident.

Osh's wife thanked the men for getting Osh to the
hospital. She and her son planned to leave immediately to
be with him. The neighbors would take care of the house
while they were gone.

The second order of business for Arne and Liv was to
return to camp to get Leidi and to retrieve the other jeep.
The men took time to pack more provisions. They borrowed
two sleeping bags to replace the ones they had used for Osh's
stretcher. When everything had been taken care of, they

climbed back into the jeep—almost reluctantly—tired from the hunt, upset over Osh's condition, and afraid that there were disappointments yet to come. The drive back to camp seemed longer than before. It was borderline sinister. In their hearts they almost knew what they would find.

As they had halfway anticipated when they reached the camp, there was no sign of the dog. The snow was so trampled from their earlier visit that it was impossible to tell whether or not Leidi had ever returned to camp. They drove as far into the forest as they could, looking in vain for the dog or her tracks. They picked up her earlier trail when she tracked the moose, but they had to leave the jeep and continue on foot because of the density of the trees and rocks.

Once they were on foot, they located and followed two trails, one made by a big bull moose, the other made by a forty-five-pound gray elkhound that was hot on its trail. Next, they found the area where Leidi held the moose at a stand—for a longer than usual time, judging from the worn encirclement of trodden snow and the angry imprints left by a nervous moose. Then they followed Leidi's new trail as she backtracked to the spot where Osh catapulted down the mountain. From there her trail led them back to camp, and it gradually disappeared into the already darkened forest.

Leidi obviously had made a decision at that point and was on her way home. No one but Leidi knew the route she would take. With night coming on, Arne and Liv had no recourse but to set up camp for the night. They would try again tomorrow to find the missing dog.

What was usually a time for good-natured teasing turned into a trial of short-tempered impatience. The campfire was all smoke and produced no heat. It succeeded in discouraging nighttime visitors from the forest, but in return, it caused the men to cough sporadically. The borrowed sleeping bags did not seem to keep them as warm as their own bags did, and the mugs of strong black coffee—meant to warm them—perpetuated their sleeplessness. When the first hint of dawn turned the whiteness of the snow to a faint pink, Arne and Liv, still exhausted, crawled out of their sleeping bags.

They spent the better part of the next day combing the area until they found themselves following their own tracks. Exhaustion was taking over where common sense once prevailed. The search came to a halt. They emptied what food they had not consumed onto the crude table that was nailed between the two big trees. The crude table was their altar in the forest. The food they emptied onto it was their offering for Leidi if she came back. They already knew that she would get no part of it for they were being watched the entire time, not by the gods of the forest, but by the creatures of the forest. The offering would be fought over and de-voured before the exhaust from the jeep had a chance to blend with the rising mist from the forest floor. Leidi would have to become as a creature of the forest to survive. The dejected men went home.

On the third day, Arne and Liv went to the hospital in Kirkenes to visit Osh. The visit was just as difficult as it had been for them to return to camp and not find Leidi. They were told by the nurse that several of Osh's bones were broken and that serious complications from severe bruising of the bone could occur. He would be in the hospital a long time and, even when he was dismissed, he would have to wear a brace and walk with crutches for months.

Osh lay in silence for a long time when Arne and Liv reported that Leidi was missing. When he did speak, it was to elicit a promise from them to continue the search for his dog. They had no choice but to promise. They left the hospital with heavy hearts, however, because they knew that future searches would be futile. Leidi was gone.

Arne and Liv often thought about Osh as they went on with their lives. They did not go hunting again, although they hounded those hunters who did go with questions about their trips. No one, it seems, reported seeing a gray dog.

Osh's wife called Arne six weeks after the accident to tell him that Osh was being dismissed from the hospital. He was hoping that his friends would come after him and take him home. Arne told her that of course they would. They were as eager as his family was to have him home.

Arne and Liv could hardly believe Osh's cheerfulness when they entered the hospital waiting room the next day. Osh would have met them in the parking lot if his nurse had not insisted that he remain in the wheelchair in the waiting room until his friends arrived. Arne finally signed Osh's discharge papers and pushed him in the wheelchair to the parking lot. Osh had little difficulty adjusting the brace on his leg and maneuvering himself, backside first, into the waiting car.

The first thing Osh said as they began the trip home was, "Leidi fikk Grom's valper i dag. Vi drar i morgen for a finne henne." He was certain, "Leidi had Grom's litter today," and his plans were, "We'll go tomorrow to find her."

It took three weeks for Osh to learn to hobble around
with the use of crutches and the brace on his leg. One of the
first things he did was to coerce Arne and Liv into taking
him to their hunting camp. The drive up to the camp was
beautiful. The mountain was awakening from a long winter
of snow and ice. Brooks ran full. There were bare spots in
the snow where the moose had dug down to reach the lichen
that covered the forest floor. The big animals seemed to
know that the hunting season was over. Many of them
could be seen in the distance, the cows heavy with the calves
they would drop in late spring.

As soon as they pulled into the clearing, Osh got out of
the jeep and hobbled over to the crude bench and table that
had been nailed between the trees several years before. The
bench had served more as a loading dock than a dining table
and, more recently, as an altar to Leidi. Osh
sat down on the bench to adjust the brace
on his leg before their trek into the forest.
He winced with pain as he swung his leg
upon the bench.

As Osh reached
for the straps that
bound his crippled
leg, his eyes
focused on a
crude sign.
KRAEVIES BIENJE. He
sat in stunned silence. Arne and
Liv, thinking that Osh was overcome with
emotion, stood quietly. They were ready for

the hike and had braced themselves for the impending
disappointment. KRAEVIES BIENJE. Osh read the sign
again. "Leidi!" he shouted.

Arne and Liv turned, not knowing what to expect.
They could not believe what they saw. Obviously there had
been a visitor to their camp. There above the table, nailed to
one of the trees, hung a wooden sign. The message was half
burned and half etched in a primitive manner on the jagged
board. The words were unfamiliar–KRAEVIES BIENJE–
but a very familiar drawing, the outline of what was unmis-
takably meant to be a gray elkhound, was above the words.
Along the bottom of the sign, almost as an afterthought,
were smaller but identical dog outlines–five of them.

The excited hunters could not make out the words on
the sign. It was not Norwegian. It was not the English they
had learned in school. The only thing it could be was one of
the Sami dialects. The nearest Sami village was on the other
side of the mountain. Leidi could not have gone that far.
That is almost 50 km away! Yet someone was trying to tell
them something! Someone who knows this is their camp!
Someone who has seen them with a dog! Someone who
knows where Leidi is!

The snow was still deep up there. The ridge of the
mountain was covered with treacherous ice from the inter-
mittent thawing and freezing this time of the year. It would
be virtually impossible to go over the mountain to reach the
village except by sled–or snow mobile. Even then it would
be a two-day journey. The men wondered aloud, "How
long has the sign been here! Does it really mean that someone has seen Leidi and five puppies!"

After much excited deliberation, the three men decided
that the message had to be from the Samis in the village.
Even if the dog is not Leidi, it might be a gray elkhound that
belongs to another hunting party. Hunters were always
willing to help out one another. It was settled. They would
go.

Osh thought it would be easier to cross over the mountain at the passes instead of going around because of thawing
and flooding in the valleys—the same decision made by Leidi
two months earlier. In their discussion, none of the men ever
raised the questions, "Should we?" or "Could we?" It was
always, "When we go." Pulling the ever-present hunting
knife from its sheath on his leg, Osh carved the word LEIDI
on the sign. The excited party loaded their gear into the jeep
and headed to town with the four-wheeler in high gear.

Osh wanted to leave at once. It was all Arne and Liv
could do to convince him to wait until daybreak the next day
before starting out. There were important preparations to be
made, precautions to take. They spent the rest of the day
getting ready. They trussed a snowmobile on the top of each
jeep, much the same way they had transported Osh into
Storskog after his accident.

Arne and Liv crammed both jeeps with camping
supplies. To top it all off, Osh insisted on bringing a crudely
fashioned wooden box. The unusual thing about the box
was that it had slats spaced about two inches apart on one
side. The remaining three sides were solid. With a knowing
smile—and Liv's help—Osh tied the mysterious box in place
on top of the other supplies.

Needless to say, none of the men required an alarm clock to awaken them the next morning. Just as the first inkling of dawn glinted from the far snowcapped mountain, the two jeeps could be seen swerving and sliding up the mountain. There was snow as always on the ridge, but the cold did not matter. Spring was in the air. The day was full of adventure and excitement.

And just as the sun slithered behind another mountain, the jeeps sputtered and stalled. The tired men made camp and called it a day. It was time to let the snowmobiles down from their perches where they were suspended like huge yellow birds. The jeeps would be left to rest in camp while the snowmobiles took over.

The next day the men climbed into the waiting snowmobiles and headed for the ridge. The snow had accumulated to great depths in the ravines that reached down from the ridge, creating great, wide superhighways for the vehicles. It took little effort on the part of the snowmobiles to top the ridge. Once on top, they were met with a fierce blast of wind, a sentry from the other side, telling them to proceed with caution.

As Arne and Liv eased the snowmobiles into the wind and down the other side of the mountain, a dense forest came into view. When they spotted the reindeer standing among the trees, they knew the village was nearby. They smelled the smoke before they saw it. It lay like a halo over the small, wooden houses. It was with great effort on the part of the hunters to contain their excitement as they rode into the Sami village on the other side of the mountain.

Puc

THE SAMI PEOPLE WHO LIVE IN PERMANENT villages lead an easier existence than their nomadic fore-fathers who subsisted as hunters and gatherers. The grassy knolls in the forests are as lush with berries and wildlife now as they were when the forests first emerged. The villagers still take advantage of nature's offerings and pick many liters of berries for drying and for jams. They stock up during the summer months in preparation for the savage winters that seemingly last forever.

The snow more often than not is higher than the windows, sometimes reaching the roof lines. Nor is it unusual for the snow to blot out an entire village so that its location can be determined only by a pattern of stovepipes that peep like periscopes from the white sea of snow. When supplies begin to dwindle and run out, the people begin to worry about feeding their families and yearn for the spring thaws. In that respect, through no fault of their own, they live a rather primitive existence.

Although Osh, Arne, and Liv had never visited the village, they knew where it was. They occasionally had encountered some of the men at the trading centers where many people go to barter for supplies. Smoke from the morning fires betrayed the village's existence where it lay hidden among the trees. The men followed the acrid odor of the wood fires. Their eyes itched from the low-lying smoke. The smoke led them to a well-worn path into the village, passing first the empty church and then the school.

The village was at its most quiet time. The children were in school. The men were with their herds or in the process of getting ready for the move to coastal pastures for better grazing. A few women could be seen doing a variety of chores, such as working on reindeer skins that were stretched across frames, cooking over open fires, or grinding

grain for mush for the next meal. Although the temperature
was cold, the mere thought of an end to the harsh winter
brought the families out of their houses. A few old-timers
stood out in the bleak sun, passing the time of day.

Osh, Arne, and Liv stopped long enough to ask the
group of old men for information, but the men just shrugged.
They obviously did not understand a word of the questions
Osh asked. Several stray dogs barked at them and then went
slinking into the shadows. When the hunters figured that
they were about in the middle of the village, they parked the
snowmobiles near a snow bank and began to walk through
the village.

Curiosity got the best of the group of older Sami men.
They scattered to spread the word that there were strangers
in the village. Soon a larger group of people gathered to
look. They smiled, shook their heads, and conjectured
among themselves as to what the strangers wanted. Osh
caught their attention by drawing an outline of a dog in the
snow. He made sure to point out that the dog's tail curled
up over its back and its pointed ears stood erect instead of
hanging down. The faces of the Samis lit up with understanding and they pointed off into the far corner of the
village. The hunters left their snowmobiles behind and
began to walk hurriedly in the direction of the pointing.

It was not long before the hunters heard the familiar
yapping of puppies coming from behind one of the houses.
Osh ran toward the sound, thinking it was almost too good
to be true. And it was. His hopes faded when he saw a
half dozen nondescript puppies playing in a puddle of mud.
One of the stray dogs that had barked at them earlier was

lurking nearby. It may or may not have been the sire of the puppies. Obviously, not much importance was placed on the breeding of purebred dogs in this village.

The distant sound of a handbell being rung with enthusiasm broke the silence. School was over for the day. There was excitement in the air. The hint of spring was a signal for the children to stay outside instead of seeking warmth and seclusion in their rustic houses.

There are no telephones in the village, not even a town crier, but the children already had word that there were strangers in town. The communication network among the close-knit villagers is baffling to outsiders.

Several of the noisy children discovered the parked snowmobiles and began to examine the bright yellow vehicles. They fingered the supplies, the backpacks, and especially the strange slatted box that was tied to the top of one of the snowmobiles. Other children were meandering along the slushy path, slowly overtaking the visitors.

One boy stood alone, looking at the three strangers. Suddenly he took off running between the houses, intentionally bypassing the men. As he approached what was apparently his own house, a furry streak of lightning ran to meet him. The boy scooped up an exuberant puppy into his arms and raced into the house, nearly tripping over an older dog that was dozing by the stoop. Four other bundles of gray fur set up a howl of excitement because the boy was home now and would play with them just as soon as he finished his chores—just as he has done every day since he discovered them in the pulka and his papa had given him the responsibility of their care.

When Leidi first came to this house, it had taken only two days for her to figure out that the boy was the one who would bring food out to her. She immediately made peace with him and trusted him with her puppies. While Leidi ate the mush that the boy placed in a bowl for her, she would let him play with the puppies. He seemed to favor the one with the white star on its chest. He often took it inside the house and let it romp on the floor with him. He taught it to shake hands and to fetch things that he threw.

The man knew the boy was becoming too attached to the puppy for his own good, but the puppies' yapping and excitement when the boy came home from school was a sure sign that he was taking good care of them. That was the reason the puppies were excited when the boy came running home.

The hunters heard the sudden outburst from the puppies. This time the sound was unquestionably familiar—the voice of gray dogs. It was music to their ears. Osh, Arne, and Liv hurried in the direction of the sound. Osh was not prepared for what happened next. Up ahead was a small frame house, just like the other several dozen houses that surrounded it. Yet, somehow, this one was set apart. There was a wooden frame set by the stoop. On it was stretched a reindeer skin that had been scraped smooth and dried so that only the strong hide remained. The reverse side of the skin carried the heavy reindeer coat, a luxurious throw rug in gray, tan, and white tones.

Frames used for stretching and preparing the skins could be seen outside all of the houses in the village. The reindeer were not killed for their pelts, however. They were killed when the family needed meat. The pelt, like many of the other parts of the animal, was utilized for making clothing, rugs, and harnesses.

On the other side of the door of the little house where the gray puppies were playing was a pulka. Long, leather harness straps of reindeer hide lay in the slushy snow. Evidence indicated that they had been the object of a fierce tug-of-war—and not by reindeer. Osh's eyes focused on the gray mat on the...no, not a mat—a gray dog!

"Leidi!" shouted Osh. The older dog focused her eyes onto the shadowy figures that were approaching in front of the bright sun, but she did not move. She had dreamed so many times of the hunt with Osh, only to waken to someone else's voice. "Leidi!" It came again. Reality reached the dog as a familiar scent intermingled with the familiar voice. Tears streamed down the faces of all three men as master and dog, after those long, difficult weeks, were reunited.

Only after Leidi stopped licking his face did Osh remember the puppies. He glanced around for them just in time to watch them scramble toward a slightly built whiskered man who was walking toward the house. The man's knowing blue eyes took in the situation and he understood exactly what was taking place. Each man, in turn, exchanged a quick nod of acknowledgment with the Sami man. It was obvious that the man lived here. He showed no real surprise to see the hunters. He almost acted like he was expecting them.

Without a word Osh turned his attention to the puppies. The four of them were as much alike as identical twins—in this case, quadruplets. They exemplified all the correct breed characteristics of the gray elkhound. They were all miniatures of their sire, Grom, each one of them a potentially good hunting dog. He would keep the best for himself and sell the others for a great many kroner.

"Puc," said the Sami man when he was within a few feet of the group. "Puc." He glanced toward the house. A slight movement could be detected from behind the smoky glass of the window, but there was no response to his call. "Puc!" he called a third time and there was a hint of agitation in his voice. A boy opened the wooden door and stood there. His face portrayed a look of total dejection, as downcast as though he had just lost his best friend. The man uttered Sami words, unintelligible to Osh and the others except for the word, "Puc."

The obedient boy turned around in the doorway and reached down. When he stood up and turned around again, he had a squirming, gray puppy in his arms. The puppy was licking the salty tears from the boy's face. Reluctantly the boy stepped out of the house and put the puppy on the ground with its littermates. The three men gasped! Never before had they seen a gray elkhound quite so perfect. It stood there with an air of haughtiness, knowing it was something special—taller more in attitude than in stature but heads above the others. The puppy obviously was living up to the marking on its chest, a white star, barely perceptible on the lush gray coat.

Osh just had to touch the puppy. He knelt down on his good knee, thrusting the crippled leg out behind. Making coaxing sounds and extending his hand, he called to the puppy. The puppy, acting as though it had rehearsed the scene many times, tossed its head with an arrogant assurance that is possessed only by dogs many times its age. It walked over and stood beside the boy. "Puc," said the man softly. The boy turned and went into the house alone.

Osh was so taken by the beauty and perfection of the puppy with the small, white star on its lower chest that he was oblivious to the feelings of the boy. He mistook the puppy's reticent behavior for the typical aloofness characteristic of gray dogs. Arne and Liv, however, saw the picture in a different light. They saw a puppy that had already decided who its master was and would, somehow, remain loyal to its master—the boy.

Of Leidi's five puppies, this one was destined for greatness. The other four were vying for Osh's attention. They pulled on his pant legs, chewed on the leather laces of his boots, and when that did not get his attention, they grabbed one of his mittens and ran with it. They were all gray puppies of outstanding quality, but Osh saw only one—Puc.

The Bargain

THE SAMI FAMILY DID NOT NEED NOR WANT
a dog. The herdsmen had their own dogs. There were
enough strays in the village already. It would be just
another mouth to feed and the family of four was nearly out
of grain, dried meat, and fish. Besides, everyone—animals
included—was expected to play a role in the game of survival
in this sometimes cruel arctic world. Only a small number
of the Sami people still lived as nomads, relying strictly on
their reindeer herds for their livelihood. Although the Sami
people who chose to live in the village have readily adapted
to the modern world, they exist on a frugal life-style.

The conversation between the Sami man and Osh was
going nowhere. Arne and Liv looked for an excuse to leave.
They decided to rescue the snowmobiles before curiosity got
the best of the children. The men were afraid the children
might injure themselves or the vehicles. Osh was left alone
to find a way to communicate with the Sami man. The man

just shrugged his shoulders each time Osh said something. Osh realized it was a mistake to expect the man to understand Norwegian. He tried to use the old Norse language that he learned from his grandmother. Still the man shook his head. After repeated attempts to use words failed, the two men resorted to using body and sign language.

The Sami man became impatient. He began to stomp the bare ground with his moccasin-clad feet. Osh watched as the damp ground became smooth and trickles of water oozed to the surface. The man picked up a stick. It was brittle from lying for months under a blanket of snow. He broke the end of the stick into a point and used it as a pencil to draw pictures in the soft dirt.

Humans have been expressing themselves through crude drawings for thousands of years. The oldest drawings of record are those etched on cave walls during the Stone Age. The drawings always include animals, showing man's ability to express his ideas with a few lines. Precise examples are the drawings found in Altamira in northern Spain, Lascaux in southern France, and the Alta rock drawings in northern Norway. Even though the Sami man was of a current society, he found it necessary to communicate in a proven way, regardless of how ancient its origin.

Osh could tell from the drawings that the Sami expected to be repaid for tending Leidi and her litter. Osh was more than willing and prepared to pay. In fact, he had made up his mind to give the Sami anything he wanted, just to be able to take Leidi and the five puppies home with him. What he had not expected was that the man would demand food and supplies. It was difficult for him to perceive more

value being placed on food than on kroner. The pictures that
the man had drawn, reminiscent of the ancient drawings
found in the caves, were obliterated with more foot-stomping
and oozing of muddy water.

The Sami knew that Osh understood, and he reacted
with enthusiasm. He continued with the picture-drawing
process to demand many bushels of wheat, many barrels of
fish, and smoked moose from Osh. He was being totally
unrealistic, in Osh's opinion. Osh was becoming more and
more impatient when, as though given a cue, Arne and Liv
glided up in the bright yellow snowmobiles. Three presump-
tuous children had crowded in with Arne. The other children were racing along behind, laughing and calling to their
brazen buddies.

The Sami's face lit up. That's it! Nothing else will do.
He must have one of the snowmobiles! Take it or leave it.
With much gesturing and excited verbiage, the Sami kept
smiling and patting one of the shiny vehicles. Osh groaned
when he realized what was happening.

The Sami smoothed the dirt one more time with his
small moccasin-clad feet. With the acumen of an ancient
artisan, he drew an unmistakable picture of the sleek snowmobile. He gestured with a flourish of his arms at Leidi and
the puppies and then at Osh. Repeating his theatrical bow,
he pointed at one of the snowmobiles and then to himself.
Confused over the rapidly declining situation, the three
hunters began to talk excitedly among themselves.

Osh asked his friends what they thought he should do.
They all agreed that he could buy dozens of gray elkhounds
for the price of a snowmobile. They knew that the Sami had

out-bargained Osh. They felt, in retrospect, that Osh should have handed the Sami man some money, taken the dogs, and pulled away at the very onset of the bargaining. Now they were wondering if Osh should risk further bargaining. After all, there were other gray elkhounds in the world—but, on the other hand, there was only one Leidi. Osh was already wondering if his family would forgive his extravagance. Many suggestions were made and retracted by the men, but it was too late now.

The Sami saw Osh shake his head in dismay. He took it as a signal that the bargaining was over. He reached down and picked up the beautiful puppy from the pulka where it was playing and moved toward the door of his house with an almost inaudible, "Puc."

Osh reacted in a panic when he saw the beautiful puppy about to be lost to him forever. He quickly pointed to the snowmobile with one hand and to the Sami with the other, much like the melodramatic gestures he had just witnessed. He continued the pitiable pantomiming, pointing to himself with one hand and the pulka full of puppies with the other. With a wide grin the Sami opened the door of his house and called for his family to come out. With much laughing and talking, the family began to remove the hunters' belongings from one of the snowmobiles. The stunned hunters' immediate reaction was that the entire charade had been a ploy.

Only the boy stood back. He could not bring himself to participate in the gusto that was tearing his young heart to shreds. In a state of total dejection, he would not even allow himself to reach down and pat the devoted puppy as it tugged at the strips of leather that held the boy's leggings snugly around his thin legs. The boy, like Osh, had difficulty putting a price tag on anything as priceless as the strings tied so securely around his heart. He watched with no outward emotion as those strings broke, but on the inside, he was devastated.

The three hunters stood helplessly by, watching the busy Sami family. The man drove a hard bargain. He motioned for his family, like the brash school children, to pile into the empty snowmobile that was meant for two people at the most. The Sami people may be smaller in stature but they are greater in determination—they squeezed in. The yellow transport lurched off and was swallowed immediately by the dense forest. The three hunters, mouths agape, stood in silence.

Osh had bargained for his gray dogs and lost his snowmobile. As a result, he had Leidi and her five beautiful puppies that were sired by Grom. Although each puppy would bring a handsome price, the full amount would not even come close to being enough to purchase a new yellow snowmobile.

All of a sudden the men began to laugh. They laughed until they rolled on the ground in helplessness. They laughed even harder when the puppies joined the fun and pulled on the men's boot laces. Leidi, not quite sure of what was happening, joined in with a shrill chortle, her head raised, wolflike, in the air.

Osh was the first to gain his composure. In a mimicking gesture, emulating the Sami who had just outwitted him, he motioned for Arne to back the remaining snowmobile up to the pulka. With a flourish of hands—and much help from the puppies—the men lashed the harnesses from the pulka to the vehicle. This sled would not be pulled by reindeer. It would be pulled by a yellow snowmobile. Even Old Saint Nick—or Julenissen, for that matter—would have been envious.

With the harnessing accomplished, they pushed four squirming puppies, one-by-one, into the slatted wooden box that Osh had insisted on bringing. They fit the box onto the floor of the pulka. The rest of the gear was packed in the snowmobile with Arne and Liv. Leidi would ride in the pulka with Osh and her brood. After all, the pulka had been their home first. But wait! That leaves one more puppy and that special puppy needs a name. Osh meant for everyone to hear when he said, "Come on, Puc. Let's go home!" Or, as it sounded to the old men of the village who were standing around watching, "Kom nå, Puc. La oss gå hjem!"

The old men looked at each other in confused amusement. They always told their children and grandchildren that the people from the outside were a little peculiar. If only they were here to see this spectacle. It was too late now though because the hunters were ready to pull away.

The other snowmobile was nowhere to be seen when the strange-looking entourage made its way, for the last time, past the schoolhouse and the church and headed for the other side of the mountain. Leidi was going home.

The Other Side

EVEN THOUGH SPRING THAWS SENT STREAMS of icy water down the mountain, the village remained a winter wonderland of deep snow. Paths of solid ice snaked through the village, serving as a string that laced the houses, school, town hall, and church together like ornaments on a Christmas tree. The children had trampled the snow down almost to the rocky soil that is common to this part of the world. The reindeer, pulling heavy loads for the Sami people, added more ribbons of ice that wound from the village through the forest. The Samis went about the arduous task of surviving yet another winter in their persistent progression through the centuries via their intervillage iceway system.

Arne and Liv followed the paths to the edge of the village. Once they left the village, chunks of ice not unlike miniature glaciers made progress slow as well as dangerous. They eased the snowmobile slowly through thawing areas of slush, sending a spray of icy mud over the trailing pulka each time the snowmobile bounced over a hidden hole. Osh draped the reindeer skin between himself and the vehicle to escape most of the drizzle.

Leidi lay on the floor of the pulka, content to be near Osh. The puppies in the slatted box set up a continuous yapping, perplexed at being penned in, yet obviously thrilled by the excitement of being pulled by the snowmobile. Only Puc registered resentment at being taken from his home—from his young master. The only thing that kept him from leaping out of the pulka was the fact that his mother, for reasons he did not understand, seemed perfectly content. Even his littermates were enjoying the adventure. At least he did not have to ride in the slatted wooden box with them.

Once the strange-looking assemblage headed up to the ridge, it was a smoother ride for the occupants of the pulka. There was plenty of snow left on top of the mountain for the snowmobile to dig into and pick up a little speed. The danger now was the possibility of turning over and being injured. The thawing had softened the drifts and, although the men were experienced drivers, they had never before pulled a pulka behind a snowmobile.

The three friends were pleased to have recovered Leidi and her litter, and in spite of losing a snowmobile to the Samis, they were equally pleased to be on their way home. Suddenly they were very hungry. They pulled into a clearing and made sure that they were on solid ground before they stopped. They shared a late repast of cold coffee, bread, cheese, jerky, and cookies. As guest of honor, Leidi shared the food with them before she jumped out of the pulka for

exercise and exploration. They still had a short but dangerous journey from here to their camp on the other side of the
mountain.

Osh stood up and turned to pick Puc up. He was going
to set the puppy out on the trail with his mother, but Puc
was nowhere to be found. Osh could see Leidi up ahead,
paralleling the tracks the snowmobiles had made on the way
over but not Puc. "Puc! Puc!" There was no sign of the
pouting puppy anywhere.

Osh called to Leidi who responded on command.
"Finn," commanded Osh. Not knowing what she was
supposed to find, Leidi cast a wide circle around the group
and came back with an expectant expression. The men got
out of the snowmobile, being careful to stay on the trail.
They called and called to the puppy, but there was no response. Osh became frantic. Again he commanded Leidi,
"Finn!" Leidi cocked her head, first one way and then the
other. She arched her neck and wagged her tail, making no
move to leave Osh again. "Finn," urged Osh.

Leidi gave an unexpected bark, almost a question. The
men were puzzled. Leidi kept turning her head from one side
to the other, tail wagging, looking first at Osh then at the
ground. She gave another bark and then wiggled all over at
the muffled answering bark that sounded like it was coming
from a deep well or from inside a cave. Arne and Liv made
their way to Leidi on the other side of the pulka. She barked
again, trying hard to tell them something.

Faintly, just faintly, they heard another far away bark,
but they could not tell where it was coming from. Arne
ventured a little farther from the jeep. He spotted a hole in

the deep snow which was unusual because there was nothing but clear sky above the drift. There was no possibility that something from a tree had fallen into the drift and caused the hole. Peering into the darkness of the hole, Arne heard the bewildered cry of a small animal. Grabbing shovels from the snowmobile, Arne and Liv began laughing and pushing the snow away from the hole. Leidi did her share of digging and soon an embarrassed Puc was leaping like a frog out of his dark snowy prison. The puppies in the box barked and begged to join in the fun. The men knew better than to release them in this field of snow traps.

Osh grabbed Puc by the scruff of the neck and chided him good-naturedly. Once again the men took their places in the snowmobile—with Osh in the pulka—and continued toward camp. Puc relaxed a little bit in the security of Osh's lap. Leidi chose to trot behind the pulka. She stayed on the rut it was retracing from the early morning journey to the village. She felt much better than she had felt nine weeks earlier when she was headed in the other direction. She knew she was really going home this time.

As the men drove, they made plans for the trip back to their main camp. Getting back to their temporary camp for tonight was easy compared to what they had in store once they loaded the jeeps and headed through the rough terrain. It was not far ahead of dusk when they spotted their jeeps. They had reached their destination for the night. Knowing that the four puppies would not stray far from their mother, Osh let them out of the wooden prison. They ran and barked and played, always underfoot, as the men readied their tents for the night.

Osh had no desire to go tramping in a dark forest looking for a puppy that was determined to return to its birthplace. He put the indignant Puc in the slatted box. The other puppies immediately taunted Puc who turned his head and pretended to sleep. He was tired from his fall into the drift but mainly from the uncertainty of the sudden change in his life. He had a lot to puzzle over. There was so much he did not understand.

After a meal of jerky and bread, the tired campers bedded down for the night. Leidi and the puppies curled up on the reindeer cover in the pulka. Osh shared his tent with a homesick puppy that waited until Osh was asleep before it snuggled as close as it could get to the warmth of his sleeping bag. And that is where Osh found the puppy when he wakened the next morning.

Osh was not going to take the chance of losing Puc to the forest or the snow. He cut a strap from the pulka harness and fashioned a harness for Puc. He tethered the youngster to a tree and set about helping his friends pack up for the trip to the hunting camp. With great difficulty they reloaded the snowmobile onto a jeep. It took more ingenuity than engineering to figure out how to put the cumbersome pulka on the other jeep but it had to be done. Osh had traded his snowmobile for Leidi and her litter—and the pulka, of course. He wanted to keep the pulka if for no other reason than as a souvenir. In reality, however, he felt that Puc needed it as a security blanket.

It took several hours to secure everything. Leidi and the puppies would ride in Osh's jeep, the puppies in their box, Leidi on the floor beside Osh and Puc...

One, two, three, four. The puppies were playing tug-of-war with the strap on which Puc had been tethered. The end of it was wet where the knot had once been. The needle-like teeth of the puppies had chewed through the rawhide where Osh had stripped it for tying a secure knot to hold Puc. But Puc was gone!

Arne and Liv quickly gathered the four playful puppies and stowed them in their wooden box while Osh started to search for Puc. But wait—Leidi was gone, too!

Leidi was so elated at being with Osh that she imagined they were on a hunt. She was reliving the dreams of the past nine weeks. As she cast in a wide circle from camp, she scented the trail of a moose and, head held high, took off through the forest. Fortunately the moose had circled the camp the night before and bedded down not more than half a kilometer into the forest. Leidi stalked him soon after he had risen from his night's rest. Like all good hunting dogs, once she had the moose at a stand, she signaled her master. Her shrill barking cut through the chill of the morning like a steel knife.

It was just a matter of minutes before Osh, hearing the familiar music of her voice, hobbled onto the scene—a picture he would treasure for the rest of his days. Leidi was circling the moose, keeping its attention by rushing in and out, barking, nipping, making a real nuisance of herself. The nervous moose was waiting for the right moment to make a run for it to get rid of the pesky thing that was nipping at its flanks. Every time the moose thought it had an opportunity to bolt away, an even smaller pest—Puc—would be there, bouncing and yapping.

Osh held his breath, his heart throbbing with fear and excitement. Keeping a moose at a stand takes skill and agility. Leidi was a master at it. A puppy as young as Puc, on the other hand, had neither the skill nor the agility, only the innate ability and the luck of the gods! Just one blow from one of the moose's hooves would be fatal.

Once the wind carried Osh's scent toward the moose, the big animal wheeled and was gone, not taking the time to get in a kick at its tormentors but clearing the ground just above Puc's head. Leidi sensed Osh's presence and ran to him when he called to her. She waited to be praised for bringing the moose to a stand, although she was curious that she was not permitted to pursue the animal. Close behind his mother, head held high, with an air of indifference to conceal the pride in himself for keeping the big animal in a nettle, stood Puc.

When Osh gave the puppy a pat on the head, he felt a shiver of excitement run through the young one. Or perhaps it was electricity generated from the bonding that took place the moment Osh's hand touched the puppy. Osh and his two hunting dogs—mother and son—made their way back to the waiting jeeps. Never again was it necessary to confine Puc.

The trip to the permanent hunting camp was slow but

without incident. It was too slow for Osh, however. He felt cramped in the jeep. His legs hurt. The swelling was tight against his leather leggings. The brace on his leg felt like a knife cutting into the swollen flesh. He should have told the doctor about the stubborn pains that kept stabbing his legs day and night, but he wanted to make this trip. He had to find Leidi and now he had her and her puppies.

The first thing the men saw as they drove into their camp was the sign that had been nailed on the tree over their makeshift table. Osh asked Arne and Liv to take it down and to be careful not to split the wood. KRAEVIES BIENJE. Gray dog—with five little gray dogs. He would hang the sign on the wall in his house as a reminder or, better yet, it would make a wonderful story opener to tell people how he acquired the limp that would surely be with him the rest of his life.

A New Home

EARLY SPRING WAS PERFECT CAMPING weather. The birds filled the air with music, accompanied by the drumming of a nearby waterfall. The entire land teemed with new life. There was very little snow left in the area. The streams created by the thawing above the camp had washed away all but the most shaded drifts. Colorful clumps of tufted saxifrage, moss campion, and yellow marsh saxifrage were peeping up around the boulders. The harsh winter was almost certainly behind them. It would be several months before Osh, Arne, and Liv would be planning another hunt. In the meantime they all needed a long rest, including the dogs.

Ordinarily the men would be thrilled with having to spend one more night out with Leidi and her family before the final leg of their journey would take them home. This time was different, however.

Osh had not taken the precautions that his doctor

insisted on. As a result, his legs were swollen like stuffed sausages and throbbed with every pulse beat. Osh did not complain, and he tried not to show his discomfiture, but even Leidi knew that something was wrong. She sniffed the elastic bandages that were wrapped around Osh's legs. She whimpered with the urge to pull the bandages off and lick the soreness from his legs, the same way she knew how to work a thorn or splinter from her own feet.

After watching Arne remove the sign from the tree and lay it in the bottom of the pulka for safekeeping, Osh consented to let Liv set up his tent and unroll his sleeping bag for him. The men made coffee on the primus stove. They insisted that Osh drink the steaming brew and eat a can of their dwindling rations. He took his medicine with the last gulp of coffee and zipped himself into his sleeping bag for the night. Even the caffeine did not keep him awake once the medicine took affect.

Leidi and the puppies nosed around the camp for a while, hoping to scare up a hare or, better yet, a fox—or anything that moved. They were ready for some action. Arne kept calling Leidi back to camp when she wandered too far. He wanted her to stay close by because the men were getting ready to turn in for the night.

Leidi eventually settled down on the floor of Osh's jeep with the reindeer cover for a bed. One by one the puppies joined her—all but Puc who stood by Osh's tent, waiting. Liv noticed him standing there and unzipped the flap so that he could get in with Osh. The tired puppy curled up at the foot of Osh's sleeping bag and went to sleep, dreaming of whatever it is that very young puppies dream about.

Arne and Liv sat on the old table with the primus stove between them, sharing what little warmth it put out, drinking the hot coffee, and worrying about Osh's condition. They knew that, once they were home, one of them would be taking Osh back to Kirkenes to see the doctor. The swelling was so bad that the legs of his leather pants would have to be slit before he could take them off.

They blamed themselves for bringing Osh on this trip. He probably would be all right if he had stayed home and followed the doctor's orders. By and by sleep overcame them. They turned off the stove and crawled into their sleeping bags. The lullaby of haunting night sounds—the rushing water, the hoot of an owl, a distant howl, the crackling of twigs made by the animals of the night—lulled them into a deep slumber. They slept the night through.

The men were wakened the next morning by Osh's groaning. When they looked around, they noticed that Leidi and the puppies were gone. They could tell by the sounds coming from a nearby clump of trees that Leidi was teaching her puppies to hunt birds. Leidi was a good teacher. All of the puppies that she had produced so far had turned out to be good hunters and the puppies of this litter were already showing signs that they, too, were going to be exceptional.

Osh wakened himself with his groaning. He knew before he even tried to get up that his legs were worse. He would not be able to drive home. When he tried to turn over, he noticed that Puc was sitting by his shoulder. The puppy was waiting patiently for Osh to get up and let him out of the tent. Osh managed to ruffle the puppy's fur and played with him for a few minutes. Arne unzipped the tent flap and let Puc out. Puc joined the other dogs as they ran for a short trek into the forest.

Arne and Liv helped Osh out of his sleeping bag and walked him over to one of the jeeps where he could keep his legs elevated. All of them ate a quick meal of bread, jerky, and coffee. Osh remained in his jeep while Arne and Liv folded the tents and stowed everything into the vehicles. When everything was ready, Osh called Leidi. She came running to him, followed by the puppies. They were dragging an old animal skin that they had found in the forest. Liv held his nose and said that he was glad they were not riding in his jeep.

Much to Puc's disgust, he was put in the slatted box with his littermates for the trip home. Leidi hopped into the front of Liv's jeep because there was not room for her with Osh. His physical pain was overridden by the joy of bringing Leidi and her litter home. It had taken less than an hour after they crawled out of their sleeping bags for the hunters, in their unusual-looking caravan, to leave the forest behind and head back to Storskog.

It was noon when the two jeeps pulled into the gravel lane beside Osh's house. The beep-beep of the jeeps' horns caused the puppies to yap. Leidi began a chorus of excited barking when she recognized her surroundings. Her barking excited the puppies even more. Osh's family came rushing outside to see what the ruckus was all about. Leidi ran from one to another, expressing her elation by barking, jumping, and licking their hands. She finally grabbed someone's mitten and ran with it. She threw the mitten into the air, caught it, and shook it like she was trying to shake the life

out of it. That was her way of showing how glad she was
to be home.

Osh was unable to get out of the jeep by himself. He
insisted that Arne and Liv put the box of yapping puppies
into the big pen by the shed. Then the men could   help
him. He knew that the dogs would keep up
their noisy banter until they were let out
and that no one could be heard as long as
the dogs were barking. However, he
warned Arne and Liv to wait until they
got inside the pen before they opened the
box or the puppies would escape and the
men would never catch them. Leidi was
put in the pen with her family to prevent her
from furthering the puppies' excitement with
her own antics. Once they were turned loose
inside the pen, the puppies were content to explore their new
surroundings and to play in the shallow water trough that
stood beside the shed.

Only after the dogs were taken care of would Osh
allow his wife and son to help him out of the jeep and into
the house. Arne and Liv stayed outside to unload the jeep.
There was no place to put the boat-like pulka except in the
big pen with the dogs. The men completely forgot about the
sign that was wrapped in the reindeer cover that Osh had
watched them pack so carefully in the bottom of the pulka.
Unknowingly it was put into the pen with the pulka.

When Arne and Liv finished unloading, they went into
the house to see what else they could help Osh with before
they went home to their own families. Osh's wife had

loaded the coffee table with platters of open-face sandwiches. There were slices of bread covered with sliced hard-boiled eggs, some with shrimps, cheeses, cucumber, and even caviar. There were platters of freshly baked cookies, a cake, and a pot of coffee. It would have been considered an insult for Arne and Liv to have refused the hospitality that is so much a part of the culture of the Scandinavian people. In truth, after the simple meals they had to endure in their camps, they welcomed the gracious hospitality.

After they had eaten, Osh, with tears in his eyes, thanked his friends for helping him find Leidi and her litter. TUSEN TAKK—a thousand thanks. As a token of his appreciation he offered each of the men one of Leidi's puppies. Nothing could have pleased them more! A puppy out of Leidi and Grom was priceless. Furthermore, Osh insisted that they all go out immediately and let each man take the puppy of his choice.

Arne and Liv led the way. Osh, flanked by his wife and Ola, his son—all totally sated with the delicious repast— made their way outside to the dog pen. They gasped in disbelief at what they saw. The puppies had found the reindeer cover in the bottom of the pulka. They had tugged and tugged until they had it halfway out of the sled. In the process, the cherished sign, so carefully wrapped and stowed for its safekeeping, had been upended when the cover was pulled out. The sign now leaned upright against the outside of the pulka where it had fallen out.

The sight that greeted the onlookers was worth a thousand words. There against a reindeer cover background leaned a sign that read KRAEVIES BIENJE. Gray dog.

Above the sign, standing in a perfect pose on the seat of the
pulka, stood the most perfect gray dog that any of them had
ever seen. Four puppies were still tugging at the cover but
the fifth one was standing on top of the world and only he
knew what his far-seeing eyes were searching for.

Arne and Liv knew that they had their choice of the
four puppies on the ground. That was understood. The one
on the pedestal would always belong to Osh. Overcome
by the beauty of the moment, Osh could no longer with-
stand the overwhelming feeling that he was in a dream.
The pain that was tempered by the relief of getting home
surged forward once more. When his knees buckled under
him and he slid into oblivion, it was Puc who jumped from
his perch in the pulka and ran to tend to his master.

What was to have been a joyous homecoming
turned into a sad farewell. Ola summoned a helicopter
after his father collapsed. Arne and Liv waited with Osh's
wife and son until the helicopter arrived in the field beside
the house. The paramedics checked Osh's vital signs and,
finding them stable, placed him on a stretcher. They lifted
him into the helicopter and took him once again to the
hospital in Kirkenes.

The rush of wind from the rotor blades threw dust
into the eyes of Osh's family and friends as they watched
him go. It was not the dust that caused the tears that
streamed down their faces. Their only consolation was that
Osh knew Leidi was home and that Puc was standing there
watching and waiting.

New Friends

PUC'S MOTHER AND TWO OF HER PUPPIES were asleep in the pulka. They seemed perfectly content to while away their days in the pen, aimlessly digging holes in the hopes of unearthing a bone that was buried by one of their predecessors. Sometimes they played King of the Mountain—or King of the Pulka—when one dog would jump in the pulka and try to keep the others from getting in. Or sometimes they played tug-of-war with what was left of the reindeer cover that was like a security blanket to the whole family. Leidi joined in the fun once in a while, but for the most part, she lay in the sun and watched her busy offspring and waited for someone to come—at least to bring a pan of dog food.

Leidi was getting old and fat for a hunting dog. She had not been hunting since the day Osh had his accident, although she had done some informal hunting on her own. When Osh found her and brought her back home with her puppies, she, like Osh, thought that everything would be like it was before the accident.

Osh's two friends each took one of her puppies. She did not expect to keep them around anyway. They all leave in time. But she had not seen Osh at all. Someone else feeds her and the other dogs in the pen and brings them water. In fact, she had not been out of the pen since that day many weeks ago.

Puc joined the fun now and then but he knew he did not belong in a pen. He was a hunting dog. He belongs in the forest—in the mountain where he was before the men came and brought him here. That is where he belongs. Someday he will go back to his birth home—back to the boy.

Listening to the stillness of the night, Puc knew the other dogs were asleep in the pulka, but he was too restless to sleep. He followed the fence around his prison. As he started around for the third time, he stepped into one of the holes that the others had dug in their endless search for bones. He put his nose down to sniff it out. As he was sniffing, he discovered that he could see under the fence—and the grass looked greener. Curiosity is not reserved only for cats. Puc put his head under the fence and crawled to the outside.

He trotted up to Osh's house but it was dark and still. The people in the house were asleep, just like the dogs in the pen were asleep, and like Puc was supposed to be asleep. He trotted to the barn and nosed open a door that was hanging in disrepair. Sleek little gray mice scattered in all directions. They need not worry. Puc was not so hungry that he would lower himself to the level of eating rodents. He left the barn and started up the gravel road.

Just then he scented something. Whatever it was, it was coming toward him along the fence. Puc sank to the ground and watched. The animal stopped and stood perfectly still, its head to one side. Without warning, it jumped up in the air and did a swan dive into a clump of weeds. It caught and devoured whatever it was after—probably a field mouse—and went on its way. The animal, a fox, was so intent on filling its belly that it did not see or sense Puc even though it passed within a few meters of him. The fox headed for the barn where, no doubt, it dined on mice every evening. Puc shook his head vigorously, repulsed at the thought.

The lonesome dog continued on his way, not knowing where he was but confident in what he was doing. He cut across a field and came to another house. A dog in the yard gave a warning bark and Puc made a wide circle around it. Two more dogs took up the challenge, walking stiff-legged toward him. Puc let out a menacing growl of his own and kept right on going. Knowing that he had bluffed his way out of a fight where he was clearly outnumbered, Puc decided to call it a night and headed back to the pulka. He had no trouble at all retracing his own tracks.

Just as dawn was beginning to break, he found the opening under the fence of his pen and crawled back under. He was wet with the early dew, fatigued, and hungry. He heard Leidi scratch the old reindeer cover into a more comfortable pallet and settle down on it with a deep sigh. The other two flopped over and continued their dreams. Puc went around to the back of the shed where he had burrowed out a den of his own underneath the shed. Exhausted from his first successful escape from his prison, he fell sound asleep.

"Puc! Puc!" Osh's son, Ola, brought a pan of food out for the dogs. Leidi and the other two young dogs were waiting for their daily rations, but Puc was not with them. Remembering how much his father idolized Puc and how he made Ola promise to take care of the dog, the young man almost panicked when he did not see Puc. He would never forgive himself if anything happened to that dog, although it did seem a shame for such a beautiful animal to spend its life in a pen.

Ola put the food down and walked around the shed, looking for Puc. The dog was sound asleep. Ola called to Puc and coaxed him out from under the shed with promises of food and play and hunting, inwardly knowing that he could not keep his promises. He was relieved that the beautiful gray dog was only sleeping and not sick, or at the very worst, gone.

Once Puc found a way out of the pen, there was no keeping him in. He spent the day waiting for the night. As soon as it grew dark, he slipped out again. He visited Osh's house first but it was quiet like it was the night before. He visited the barn, and, just to prove that he was as adept as the fox, he stalked a mouse. He found it easier to pounce on the mouse from a crouching position than to dive on it as the fox had done. Repulsed by the odor of the squealing varmint, he let it out from under his paw without really hurting it.

Bored with catching mice, but smug at knowing he could, Puc took off across the field. The stray dogs were

laying for him. One at a time, they challenged him and
circled around him, stiff-legged and growling. Puc drew
himself up and let the fur on his neck and back stand straight
out. With a ferocious growl, he broke into an easy trot and
ran in front of the biggest dog, cutting him off from the
others. The strays were unable to intimidate the newcomer,
so they accepted him. Once again Puc had bluffed his way
out of a fight. This time he led the pack across the field.

The four dogs spent the better part of the night explor-
ing the barns and houses in the area. There were no street
lights in the country. All of the inhabitants of the houses
and barns were sleeping, resting for what lay in store for
them with the dawning of a new day.

One barn was no different from the others until they
came to one with a peculiar scent. It had a small low door
that was close to the ground. Naturally, one of the dogs
went in because that is what doors are for. The other dogs
could hear a commotion from inside the long, low building.
The dog soon came running out, proudly carrying a squawk-
ing chicken in its jaws. Feathers flew everywhere as the
other dogs tried to take the chicken away from the thief.
They all ran toward the field, squabbling over their trophy.
Puc eventually grew tired from the excitement and more
hungry for dog food than for chicken feathers. He made his
way back to his pen and slipped into his den under the shed
shortly before dawn. In a matter of minutes, he was sound
asleep.

As usual, Leidi and the others were up with the sun,
barking for their food—the highlight of their day. Even their
noisy barking did not waken Puc. When Ola brought the

dog food, he was puzzled that Puc was missing again. As was the case yesterday, he put the food down and walked to the back of the shed. Sure enough. There was Puc, sound asleep under the shed. With more promises, he wakened Puc and coaxed him out from under the shed. Although Puc was sleepy and tired, he was extremely hungry. He gobbled his food down in seconds. Ola knew that a dog with an appetite like Puc's was a healthy dog, and Ola went on to his job without another thought.

Puc resisted the attempts of his littermates to get him to play or to help them with their endless digging. He spent much of the day asleep in his den so that, when dusk fell, he was under the fence and gone. He followed his usual course. He played cat and mouse in the barn. He expertly landed a big paw on a mouse that peeked out from behind an old feed sack. This time he picked the critter up in his teeth, being careful to bare his lips to keep from touching it. Then he dropped the squealing mouse without so much as breaking through its velvety gray coat. He knew now that a meal was his for the taking if he ever got hungry enough to eat something so repulsive.

His dubious friends were in the field waiting for him. In a show-off manner, he jumped a ditch with nonchalance and sauntered past them. They raced in circles in a friendly game of bite and run, much different from their initial confrontation three nights ago. Puc was from one of the best bred litters in all of Norway, a misfit in a pack of stray dogs. Sharing in their enthusiasm, if not in their questionable pedigrees, Puc joined his newfound companions in a night on the town. They made the rounds, chasing cats, knocking over trash barrels, and finally, as though leaving the best until last, they came to the star-crossed chicken house.

As the first dog went in through the low door, the chickens began to cackle and fly around inside. The noise was deafening but not nearly as deafening as the unexpected shotgun blast and curses that surprised the unwary dogs. Whether it was the buckshot or the surprise, no one will ever know. The startled dogs scattered like the buckshot, three of them yelping loudly and running in all directions. The fourth dog, as silent and gray as the night, headed toward the forest.

Ola did not sleep well that night. He was concerned that he was not keeping his promise to his father to take good care of Puc. Puc was truly the most beautiful gray dog anyone had ever seen and he deserved more than living out his life in a pen. But lately, Ola was too busy with his job to spend any time with Puc. And to make last night even more sleepless, there was a big commotion at his neighbor's house. Apparently a pack of stray dogs had been after his neighbor's chickens from the way it sounded. There was so much shooting and yelping that his neighbor more than likely had filled a couple of dogs full of buckshot. Ola thought to himself that people really ought to take better care of their dogs and not let them run loose. He finally went to sleep and, in fact, slept through the persistent ringing of his alarm clock.

The impatient barking of Leidi and the other dogs gradually wakened the young man. A furtive glance at the clock told Ola that he had overslept and would have to hurry to get to his job on time. He dressed quickly, and without taking time to eat anything for himself, he took a pan of dog food out to the pen. As luck would have it, and as had been the case the last few days, Puc was not with the rest of the dogs. "Puc! Puc!" Oh, well. Ola reasoned to himself that the sullen dog was probably under the shed asleep. At the moment, his job was more important than coaxing a sleepy dog out from under a shed. He would definitely spend some time with Puc after work. It might be later this weekend before he had the time to spare, but he definitely would do it this weekend. He set the pan of food inside the pen and left quickly. Leidi and the other dogs swallowed the food greedily, enjoying the extra portion.

It was Saturday afternoon before Ola realized that he had not seen Puc for several days. The dog was never with the other dogs when he took the food out each morning. He assumed that Puc was still asleep.

Ola panicked when he looked under the shed and discovered that Puc was gone. He ran back to the house and telephoned Arne. He asked him to help look for the young dog. Arne promised Ola that he and Liv would go up to the hunting camp and search the area.

Early the next morning the men stopped at Osh's house
and retrieved the old wooden sign from the dog pen where it
had lain ever since the puppies had pulled it out of the pulka.
They planned to nail it back where they first saw it —over
the makeshift table in camp. Maybe another hunter would
see the sign and look for the missing dog. Liv would chisel
the word PUC into the sign after they nailed it back to the
tree.

Hungry Wolves

THE FOREST WAS PREPARING FOR WINTER. IT laid in a soft floor of moss to take care of the reindeer and moose. The carpet was spongy to the step and allowed the animals to move about in total silence. To compensate for being unable to hear an approaching enemy, the animals' keen senses of smell enabled them to avoid confrontations with their assailants which were, for the most part, other animals. Occasionally a sly adversary moved downwind from what promised to be a feast. In that case, the victim's acute senses were ineffective and a noisy chase ensued. The animals would run up and down, back and forth, across and over, snarling and breaking brittle branches in the onslaught. Other animals stood spellbound and watched the chase. Some hid. Some paced nervously, and some went on grazing, accepting nature's law of survival of the fittest.

As autumn faded away, leaves and twigs covered the mossy carpet, making the slightest movement a crackling signal of life, telling the whole forest when even the smallest of God's creatures moved in search of food. The mountains were already clothed in patches of new snow which meant that the forest floor would soon add a blanket to its twice-carpeted floor.

Food was becoming increasingly difficult to find, especially for the carnivore. A pack of gray wolves moved into the area, stalking near the edges of the forest. The wolves preferred to catch an unwary deer or other small animal off-guard and chase it into the open where the wolves had a distinct advantage. The wolves had, much to the dismay of the Samis, ravaged a herd of reindeer that was brought down to the fields to graze. With winter close at hand, the Samis were moving their herds back to the village on the other side of the mountain where they would be protected for the winter.

It was during this time of the year that Puc ran from the chicken house melee. The sound of the gun did not frighten him, but the anguished yelping of his outlaw buddies did. Whether consternation over the incident sent him scurrying to the forest for his own safety or whether he had already decided not to go back to his pen with Leidi and his littermates is uncertain. The fact remains that he headed for the forest.

He zigzagged his way across the fields, leaving the chicken house, his stray companions, and the security of his pen farther and farther behind. Instinctively he cast away from a direct path, but the forest and mountain beyond were never out of his sight or mind. Puc was built for the arduous work of hunting. He had the agility to jump over logs and streams without changing the rhythm of the pace he had chosen, much like the cadence of a marching band in a long parade. However, growing up in an enclosure had not given his body the opportunity to muscle to its full potential. He began to tire.

After several kilometers, with a misty dawn creeping slowly but surely overhead, Puc reached the edge of the forest. He filled his stomach with icy water from a stream to satisfy the immediate hunger pangs that reminded him that there was no one to set a pan of dog food out for him. The hunger pangs were replaced with stomach cramps from drinking the icy water. He needed to rest.

A huge tree had fallen across several smaller trees, downing them by sheer force. Puc crawled through the snarled branches and made his way under the crisscross of tangled limbs until he was well hidden from the world. He pushed into a low spot under the huge trunk and there, in the safety of a leaf-covered hole, he slept soundly for the better part of the next day.

When Puc awakened, the tree had literally come to life. Its branches, still green, were swaying as birds pecked away at its rotting trunk, pecking and eating, pecking and eating. A busy squirrel, unaware of the sojourner, scurried back and forth on the fallen trunk, picking and devouring some of the last berries of the summer, picking and eating, picking and eating.

Puc was hungrier than he had ever been. He watched the squirrel for a few minutes and decided that sometimes a dog had to do what a dog had to do. He lurched at the squirrel like he did the mice in the barn. The surprised squirrel chattered a profanity to his attacker, ran up a tree, and sat out of reach of the dog, chattering incessantly. The birds, startled by the surprise attack on the squirrel, abandoned the tree without so much as a backward glance, leaving it very dead and deserted.

A sound in the leaves caught Puc's attention. He cocked his head, lurched toward the sound, and brought a paw down on a field mouse that was dining on dried seeds that it found among the crumbling leaves. Puc's first meal as an outlaw in the wild kingdom was far from satisfying.

Puc felt the safety of the forest surround him as night fell. The hungry wolves lifted their voices to the moon in protest. Without realizing what he had done, Puc threw back his head and joined in their mournful song. The resulting silence was ominous. Momentarily the wolves repeated their howls, tentatively at first, then full chorus. They sensed an intruder. Sooner or later they would find him.

Puc worked his way deeper into the forest. He picked up the scent of a moose and, not really knowing why, he followed it for a while. He had a feeling that he knew what he was doing, an intuitive feeling that he had done this very thing before. The trail ended abruptly on the spot where the moose had met its demise. Luckily for Puc, the hunters were careless and did not dispose of the waste as they should have after emptying their kill. Puc feasted until he could scarcely move.

Puc was but one step ahead of the wolves. They, more than likely, smelled the blood of the slain moose even from a greater distance than he had. Their goal was to find food whether it was moose or an inexperienced dog. Puc moved on.

A twig snapped. Puc whirled around. The night was still. Nothing moved—not even the yellow-green eyes that reflected the moon. The two animals stared at each other, one still in his primeval state, the other a product of man's attempt to domesticate primeval dog.

Puc stood his ground. His body was drawn up to its extended height, his hackles giving him an added dimension. He tightened his lips into a snarling expression, his gleaming white teeth appearing even more menacing in the moonlight. His ruse worked with the strays. Maybe it would work with this marauder. Puc stared intently for a few more minutes. With a low rumbling growl, he started stiff-legged toward the wolf. When he was within lunging distance, he whirled and took off at a confident pace in the other direction.

There was no sound behind him. Puc did not know whether or not he was being followed. He half expected the entire pack of wolves to appear from behind every tree. He was not afraid; however, he was intelligent enough to know his limitations, and he was intelligent enough to know that the wolves knew his limitations. He was certain that his whereabouts had been communicated to the rest of the pack by now. He would be safer by staying ahead of them instead of trying to hide from them.

Another scent clouded the air. It was not of a wolf, not of a moose, not even of another dog. This was human scent. It was not Ola or even Osh, although he barely remembered Osh's scent. Puc's subconscious told him to beware of humans. Coincidentally, the scent led in the same direction that Puc had decided to take. He followed it, air-scenting with his head held high so that he could notice movements that were made, movements too stealthy to be heard. The trail led up and down, into and out of a clearing, around a clump of trees, on and on for several hours.

When the scent finally led into a little clearing, Puc decided to stop for a rest. He found a hole under a log, a den once occupied by another fugitive of the night. He would never know that Leidi once slept here when she, like Puc, was in transit; nor did he remember being here as a very young puppy. He needed time to rest, to sleep, to decide what to do. He did not know where he was going nor, for that matter, where he had been. He was so giddy that he even felt like he had been here before, like he was going home. He went to sleep to the distant sound of baying. He stifled the urge to return the mournful call.

Puc felt safe under the log, but he did not sleep as long this time. He still had much of the day ahead of him when he awakened. The full meal had helped immensely, and he was not as tired or giddy. The pads of his feet were beginning to toughen and were not as sore as they had been. He nosed around the clearing. He discovered where the humans had slept a few days ago, the same human scent he had followed. He found the offensive odor of petrol where their vehicles had been parked. He sniffed where they had dropped food. There were no crumbs on the ground because the ever-present mice and birds picked the area clean of crumbs.

There seemed to be a scent of food coming from higher
up. Puc stood on his hind legs and put his front legs on a
smooth plank that was wedged in between two trees. On
top of the table that it formed, there were ants swarming
over a piece of bread. With a swipe of his paw, Puc knocked
the bread to the ground. The ants had fallen hither and
thither when the dry bread hit the ground. With a gulp, Puc
swallowed the morsel. It was much tastier than the offensive
rodent that he had seen earlier would have been.

Puc jumped upon the table-like structure to make certain
that there were no other tasty bits to eat before he started the
next leg of his journey. He sniffed all around the top of the
table. He sniffed at the piece of smooth board that was
nailed to one of the trees that supported the table. If Puc

could read—and, of course, he could not—he would have
recognized the message: KRAEVIES BIENJE. Below the
message someone had hurriedly carved in the name LEIDI.
On the same board there was an outline of a dog shaped just
like himself with five smaller ones at the bottom of the sign.
One of the smaller outlines had a circle around it and under
the words KRAEVIES BIENJE someone had hurriedly
carved in the word PUC.

Puc sprawled out on the table. He liked being up high
where he had the advantage of seeing before he was seen. It
made him feel special, like he was in charge. He felt a
certain affinity for this place. If it were not for the wolves, he
would hang around here for a while. But yet, there was that
feeling that he was being drawn up the mountain by an
unknown force. He would have dozed in the quietness of
the clearing except that the distant howling had ceased.

The Small Wolf

PUC SPENT THE REST OF THE DAY ROAMING around the hunting camp. There was always the persistent feeling that he was on familiar territory. He kept searching for something—he knew not what nor where. Just for the purpose of suppressing his instinctive urge to hunt, he followed the scent of a moose into a clump of trees. He deserted the trail to catch a small, startled animal that made a run for cover, too late to escape Puc's powerful jaws. Puc would have been corrected severely by Osh for leaving a moose scent in favor of satisfying his own hunger but, on the other hand, if Osh had been here, Puc would not have been so hungry.

Puc left the animal remains in the clump of trees where he had devoured the critter and made his way back to the hunting camp and his den of last night. He napped on a full stomach and dreamed of another day in another life when he and Leidi brought a moose to stand somewhere near here.

Osh had been very proud of them. Puc's dream was so real that he could feel the draft of air and the vibration of thundering hooves as the moose jumped over his head and pounded away. But the pounding became too real and Puc woke with a start.

Dozens of reindeer were milling around in the camp. They would have trampled him if he had not been in a hole under a huge log. And then he heard the gnashing and pulling and tearing and smelled the pungent, warm and sticky smell of blood as a wolf killed a reindeer. Puc lay quietly, wanting to be rid of the place. A hunting dog would never kill a reindeer. The yellow-green eyes that he saw, seemingly suspended above the carnage, confirmed Puc's realization that the entire pack of wolves had been in on the kill. The hackles on the back of his neck rose as he eased out of his den.

Puc decided to make a run for it, thinking that the wolves would be concentrating on their kill. They were not likely to pursue him if they had a feast already on the ground. Just as Puc jumped over the log, he felt a pain that paralyzed him in mid air. He was jerked by an unseen pair of jaws and slammed to the ground. A shot split the cold night air and the yellow eyes in the dark were gone. Puc lay on the ground near the log as though he would never rise again. Next to him lay a gaunt gray wolf which would never kill another reindeer, or, for that matter, any other animal. The gunshot out of the dark had hit its mark.

Puc's mind was whirling, spinning, sometimes coming to a halt and then the whirling would start all over. Each time the spinning slowed he thought he heard voices. When his thoughts did climb to the surface and stayed there, he was positive there were humans in the camp. He could not lift his head. His entire body was one huge, throbbing pain. He felt the ground wet and sticky under him—and he could smell his own blood. Suddenly his senses were gone and the night went with them.

Morning had a difficult time making itself known. A heavy, drizzling rain kept pushing it back into the dark. The reindeer were grazing in the clearing beside the camp, calm as though nothing had happened. A man and boy were walking toward the spot where Puc lay behind the dead wolf. The man kicked at the dead wolf, reaffirming that there was no life left in it. He directed the boy to get on the other side of the lifeless animal and help him tie a rope around its carcass so that it could be strung up to a tree and gutted.

The boy, Petter, reluctantly obeyed. When he stepped around the dead wolf, his moccasin-clad foot stepped against something soft and spongy but not quite like the lichen that matted the ground in this area. "Pappa!" he cried in dismay.

The man, startled by the anxiety in his son's voice, ran for the gun he had laid on the old table. He ran back to where his son was kneeling. There, stretched out behind the dead wolf that had helped kill one of his reindeer was a smaller wolf—at least it appeared to be a smaller wolf. In the half dark of the early morning, it looked like it had the same color—that which was not covered with blood. It had the same prick ears, the same long tail—well, maybe not as long. It had the same big head and vicious teeth—well maybe not quite.

Big wolf or small wolf, the man would kill it so that it would never again bother his herd. He raised his gun to shoot the semi-conscious gray animal and ordered his son to move out of the way. "Nei, Pappa!" cried Petter. "Det er ikke en ulv!" Petter kept repeating softly, "Det er ikke en ulv— it's not a wolf." He continued to kneel over the animal, stroking its head, looking for vital signs of life. Puc opened his eyes and looked at his protector. He closed his eyes. It was just another part of his dream—the boy from the past.

The drizzle of cold rain had changed to snow. This time of the year the weather was as unpredictable as was the shape of one of the fluttering snow flakes. A foot or more of heavy, wet snow could fall at one time, hiding landmarks, and making travel next to impossible. There was already new snow in the mountain. The man knew it was time to drive the herd back to the village before the snow made the mountain impassable.

He should have told his son to move out of the way while he put the wounded animal out of its misery — whether it was a wolf or a dog. No animal deserved to suffer. If he had gone ahead and shot the wounded animal, they would be on their way by now. The wolf pack would not be likely to attack again so soon. The reindeer were calmed down enough to make it to the top of the mountain by nightfall. From there he could summon help from the village if the wolf pack followed. They should have moved on.

Pappa was worried about his son. Petter was quiet and withdrawn, grieving over giving up the gray puppy a few months ago. Pappa knew now that he should have let Petter keep the puppy when the hunters came and took the mother dog and all the puppies. Petter was still upset.

As Pappa paced back and forth in the clearing, he noticed that the sign he had put up above the old table was back. There was a circle around one of the puppy drawings that Pappa had made at the bottom of the sign. If the hunters cannot keep track of their gray dogs any better than losing them all the time, he thought, they do not deserve to have the beautiful dogs. If he finds another one, he will bargain for the other snowmobile. That will teach them to take better care of their dogs.

Petter went to the tent they had been living in and retrieved a water container and an old reindeer skin. He dipped the container full of icy, cold water at the nearby stream and carried it to where the wounded dog lay. Petter began to rinse the blood from the dense coat of the dog and to cleanse the gash on its flank. The animal seemed to respond to Petter's gentle touch for it began to stir and was watching the boy's every move. It winced when Petter tried to clean the area on its flanks where all the blood seeped into its heavy coat. The boy gently pulled the dog onto the old reindeer skin to make it more comfortable and to get it out of the bloody mud in which it was lying.

Petter had spent so much time nursing the wounded dog that it was too late in the day to head up the mountain with the herd. They would spend another night in camp and get an early start tomorrow. Meanwhile, Pappa set about building a small fire in their tent. The tall tent of reindeer hide was supported on four strong poles, arranged in such a way as to have a smoke hole at the apex where the four poles came together. Building the fire directly under the smoke hole caused a draft that pulled the smoke out the top. In earlier times this provided a convenient way for Sami people to smoke their meat when they had fresh meat to preserve. The fire would help stave off the wolves if the pack decided to attack the herd again tonight. Pappa and Petter both needed something warm inside them to help ward off the onslaught of cold weather. Pappa would fix something for them to eat.

The man had just about decided to tell his son he could take care of the dog until it got well; then he would have to let it go. Suddenly he heard a yell of excitement from his son. "Pappa! Pappa!" He ran to see what the boy wanted.

Petter had managed to get much of the blood stain from the thick gray coat of the dog. In spite of having just been bathed in cold water from the stream, the animal's coat looked quite dry. The tail which had been stretched out almost as long as a wolf's tail was now curled up over its back. Its eyes were dark, not the yellow-green evil eyes of the wolves that glared through the night. "Se, Pappa!" The excited boy held the dog's head up away from its gray chest and told Papa to look. There, gleaming in its own whiteness on the gray chest, was a perfect star. The two looked at each other. Their gasps exploded with one sound, "Puc!"

That one word caused the curled tail to flicker. Just hearing his name made Puc realize he was no longer dreaming of that other life. This was real. He joined their excitement with a loud yap. Even though each wag of his tail hurt his aching body, he could not keep it still. He wanted to get up, to run and play, to find something to throw in the air, something to shake hard. He wanted the boy to hug him, to scratch him behind the ears—to make the pain go away.

Together Pappa and Petter carried the gray dog, cradled in the reindeer skin, into the tent. They shared their meager warm meal with Puc. The rest of the day passed quickly while the father and his son lavished Puc with attention. Pappa knew that this was the missing puppy, the one that someone had circled on the sign above the table. As far as Pappa was concerned, however, the dog was not missing at all. It belonged to Petter.

After supper, in the security of the tent—as superficial as the security was— the boy and Puc slept soundly as the man kept watch over his herd. The freezing rain and snow stopped and the moon was bright. In the distance, a mournful howl broke the silence of the night. Inside the tent, a gray dog answered the howl in his dream, wincing out loud as his twitching pulled at the ugly gnashes on his backside. The boy stirred and settled again, reaching for the dog's warm body.

The man smoked his pipe in peaceful solitude. The gray dog was going to recover from the wound, and it would be all right. Petter had his dog back, and now he would be all right. Tomorrow they would head for the top of the mountain. When Papa finally got the herd back to the village,

Pappa would be all right. The prospect of enduring the approaching winter was the farthest thing from his mind. His world was all right.

Next Time

AWN CREPT INTO THE TENT AS SILENTLY AS wolves. The fire on the ground in the middle of the tent was a mound of smoldering ashes, not even hot enough to melt the frost. It would not take much heat to warm some mush for the three of them, something to stick to their stomachs for the long, slow meander up the mountain. He would put several small twigs on the ashes. It would burn down before they took the tent down.

Pappa let the boy and dog sleep as long as he dared. He watched the pair until he caught sight of a flicker of the dog's eyelids. That dog was a sly one! Trying to make the man think he was sleeping when all the time he knew the man was standing there watching. He will make a fine watch dog, not yet as cunning as the big wolf that attacked him, but that will develop with age. This dog will earn his keep. He would bet on that. "Puc," he said quietly.

Puc raised his head and looked at the man. The only indication that Puc recognized the man was that he did not growl. He tried to get up but could not make his hindquarters do what his forequarters wanted. He was able to pull his rear along the slick hair of the reindeer cover until he reached the mossy ground. The traction from the rougher surface and the moss for his claws to dig into helped him pull himself to a wobbling stand. With great difficulty, he hauled himself out the tent opening into the frosty cold of a new day.

Petter immediately sensed that Puc was gone. He groped for the furry coat, finding only the warm spot on the reindeer skin cover where Puc had slept without moving the entire night. The blood from the dog's wound left a crusty patch on the cover, a good sign that the bleeding had stopped. Petter clambered out of the snug hole he had burrowed in the heaped covers, concerned only about the dog. His puppy with the star had found him at last. He saw the hint of a smile on Pappa's face and knew that everything was all right, that Puc would not leave him again.

Before Petter could get out the tent opening, Puc came walking stiffly back in. Some of the soreness had worked out of his rear already, and he was steadier on his feet. His tailed wagged when he saw the boy. His attention, however, went to the pot of gruel hanging over the dwindling fire. Pappa could not believe that he was going to share his meal with a dog. His family would think he had gone mad. Last winter had been such a harsh one, so harsh that they had almost run out of supplies. This winter would more than likely be the same. The men in the village would ridicule him when he came back with a dog, a crippled one at that. No one ever kept a lame herding dog. He would ignore their taunts. On the other hand, maybe all his worrying was for nothing—maybe this winter would be easier.

The wolves had not shown up all night. They were gone for the time being, but wolves do not forget. They will come back to finish their interrupted meal and to mourn one of their own. They will find no trace of either, however, because scavengers of the night had gleaned everything that was edible. Only the strange offensive scent of fear lingered.

The trio—Pappa, Petter, and Puc—finished the simple, but warm, meal quickly. With few words and no need to give his son instructions, Pappa quickly dismantled the tent with Petter's help. They had the routine worked out perfectly. Either one of them could have done it alone. The tent became a gierehtse. The tough hide cover was lashed to the poles, much like a sling or drag. The gierehtse served as the carrier for all the rest of their belongings, a technique used by people everywhere for many centuries. The gierehtse was then harnessed to a reindeer that served as a pack animal for the jaunt back to the village. The preparations took less than half an hour.

Pappa did not know if Puc could make it all the way back to the village on foot. The nasty gash on his flank would take several weeks to heal. The wolf would have killed the dog if Pappa had not interfered. Fortunately for Puc, the wound was superficial and did not penetrate the muscle.

Pappa decided to let the dog ride on the gierehtse with Petter, but Puc did not understand what the man and boy were trying to get him to do. Petter climbed onto the dragging contraption and called to Puc. The pack reindeer was already on the move, causing the dragging poles to grit along the rocky terrain, digging at the moss. Petter hopped off the frame and held the old cover in front of Puc, coaxing him toward the frame. In exasperation, Petter tossed the cover back up on the frame, picked up the aching dog, and laid him on the cover. Petter crawled up behind Puc to keep him from jarring down the back side of the frame. It was in this manner that the reindeer herd, accompanied by the man, the boy, and the dog, slowly wended its way toward the mountain.

Puc and Petter slid off the bouncing drag periodically to stretch their legs. The rut left by the poles grew fainter and fainter as the herd progressed upward. The temperature continued to drop. They would soon be in freezing temperatures, gusting wind, and from the looks of it, snow. The surface of the trail leading upward was almost barren rock. Even though there was very little for them to eat, the reindeer continued to graze as they climbed, closer and closer to the ridge that overlooked their village.

Back at the hunting camp, there was no indication that the Samis had been there. They left no trappings other than the inedible remnants of the slain wolf and reindeer. The round circle of earth on which the fire in the tent had burned for days was long since cooled. Pappa had kicked wet moss over it to hide its ashes. The simple existence of the Samis did not include Styrofoam cups, paper plates, or aluminum

cans, things that their more affluent relatives who had taken
jobs in the mines and factories were accustomed to using.

Cleaning up camp was as simple as converting the tent
into a gierehtse and kicking out the fire. It would have been
impossible to disguise the fact that a herd of reindeer had
recently grazed in the area. But there was no reason to hide
their existence. The tame reindeer herds were accepted as
part of the environment. Even the hunting dogs were
taught to ignore them. Unfortunately, the wolves lived by
Nature's laws, not the laws made by man.

About five hours after Pappa and Petter moved out of
the camp, Arne and Liv, Osh's two hunting companions,
drove into camp in their jeep. Their hunting trip up there a
few weeks ago had been successful. This time they brought
along the young dogs Osh had given them. The dogs were
turning into excellent hunters. They already had a moose
apiece on their records. A huge bull had eluded them on
their last trip and the men wanted the dogs to have another
chance to bring it to a stand.

When the men arrived in camp and let the dogs loose,
they knew that something out of the ordinary had taken
place. The dogs went wild, barking, sniffing, and running
in circles. They immediately found the scraps of evidence
that indicated wild animals had killed something. Bit by bit
the men were able to piece together what had happened.
They reasoned that the Samis had been camping nearby on
the way back to their village with their reindeer herd. One
of the reindeer had been killed, judging from the scattered
bits and pieces of hide, hooves, and antlers. Wolves and
bears were the largest predators in the area, but bears were

scarce and the government was keeping a close count of them. More than likely, a pack of wolves had attacked and killed the reindeer.

Arne and Liv surmised that, for some reason, the Sami had vacated the area in a big hurry, probably that very morning. The rut left by the dragging tent poles was still filled with oozing water, not yet frozen. The Samis would be well on their way to the ridge with their herd by now.

The sign! If the Samis had camped here, maybe they had seen Puc. Arne and Liv ran over to the old table. The sign had not been bothered. It was just like it was when they nailed it back up last week. Before they put it up, they had drawn a circle around one of the small outlines of a puppy at the bottom of the sign to indicate that Puc was gone. They may as well leave the sign there. Someone will see it eventually—maybe the Sami man who had bargained Osh out of his snowmobile.

The young dogs were still reacting to fresh scents all around the camp. They had become used to the smell of reindeer. That did not bother them. They even knew the scent of a wolf. That made them nervous, but they knew what it was. It was the other scent that caused them to bark and pant and run in circles—another dog, one of their own.

The men thought the dogs were excited because of the wolf and the reindeer. They agreed that the best thing to do was to get them on the trail of a moose as soon as possible. The dogs would be all right once they started a trail. Just in case a bear came into the area while they were gone, they left the supplies in the jeep for security. They would be back in plenty of time to set up their tents for the night.

NINA P. ROSS

Arne and Liv were training their young dogs to hunt off-lead, looshund, as it is called. Dogs that hunt on lead are called bandhunds. Some dogs can track either way, depending on the situation, density of the forest, and the depth of the snow, for instance. In an area like the Arctic where the forest is sparse, the hunters often use looshunds. As the men walked toward the clump of trees nearest the camp, they called to their looshunds.

Young dogs tend to be a bit rambunctious on the hunt. They do not bark, but they rush. Occasionally they overshoot the track. The men were certain the dogs were on the track of the big bull. The hoof marks in the soft ground were large and deep. One dog stayed with the trail, but the other dog went off at a 90-degree angle, casting too wide and losing the scent. The men decided to split up, each staying with his own dog. They knew better than to risk overexposure in the forest at night. By signal they would retreat back to camp. If, by chance, one of the dogs brought a moose to stand, everyone for kilometers around would hear the shrill barking. The other hunter would call his dog in and wait for the telltale sound of the shot before joining forces with his partner to help dress out the moose.

Arne spotted a dark form just inside a clump of bushes and took aim. He knew that the bullet would fragment if it hit branches before it hit the intended mark just behind the bull's shoulder. He tried to get closer but the shifting of the wind blew his cover. The big animal whirled and could be heard crashing through the thicket. Arne wished that he had Leidi with him. She would have held the moose at a stand for him while he took aim. The big bull would not have eluded him again!

Liv heard the evasive animal coming toward him. He could almost see the huge shovels parting the lower branches as the bull ran. Something had caused it to change its course. He did not know whether it had been Arne or one of the dogs. Liv would not take aim for fear of missing the bull and hitting his friend or a dog. The animal seemed to know that it was safe because it suddenly veered behind a boulder and was quiet. The big bull had eluded them again. The hunters, like the young dogs, had been too eager.

Arne gave the signal that would bring both men and their dogs back to camp. They had learned a valuable lesson which made the short expedition worth the effort. They logged the experience in their journals and made preparations to call it a day. They pitched their tents and, coincidentally, slept on the exact spot where Puc and Petter had slept just a short time ago—so close yet so far apart. Maybe next time.

In the Ravine

HERE ARE TIMES WHEN LOOKING DOWN the mountain from on top of the ridge is an electrifying experience. The azure blue of the sky is reflected in the icy waters of the fjord below. The scattered trees stand like black sentinels on a sterilized white sheet, waiting for a piercing wind that will snap them off like dead soldiers, covering their stiff bodies with a clean white blanket, layer upon layer, until there is nothing but stark whiteness studded with colossal boulders.

And then there are times when looking down from that height to the valley below is like looking through frosted glass. The air is so thick with rime that the world becomes a downy smudge. The ice-laden trees cannot be distinguished from hoary boulders, from emaciated animals, from shadowy crevices. Even the water in the fjords at the country's edge lies like pieces of fragmented glass, its jagged edges cutting deeply into the earth. This is what it looked like when

Pappa and Petter reached the ridge late that night.

The snow came in gales of wind, lashing at their faces. It is hard to imagine how something as soft and fragile as a snowflake, so beautiful and dependent on its fellow flakes for a continued existence, can be so brutal. Pappa and Petter covered their faces with fur-lined parkas and stuck their hands inside huge mittens of the same hide, thanks to the reindeer that had sustained the Sami people for centuries with its gifts of milk, meat, and hide. In return, the Sami man and his son were bringing the herd safely back to the village for the winter, something the man had done all his life and was teaching his son. And in the next breath, the snow had stopped.

Wise in the ways of the wolves, Pappa expected trouble before he reached the top. The pack of wolves followed at a distance, off to the left side of the herd. As the natural pathways up the mountain began to deepen, they also began to narrow, bringing the wolves into closer proximity with the reindeer. The mountain had patches of baldness where, first the glacier, then the persistent wind and snow had forbidden anything but the scraggliest of scrubs to take hold. The ravines ran like rivulets from the ridge, fanning out like giant fingerprints down the mountain.

Year in and year out, after a winter of heavy snow, the ravines filled with the rushing waters of the spring thaw, washing them clean of the debris of the warm summer and gentler winds. There was nothing left on this baldness for the herd to graze. With nothing to eat and with Pappa and Petter urging them on, the young, inexperienced reindeer became nervous and difficult to control. The older cows and bulls continued, unfaltering, upward. A young reindeer from this spring's crop began to panic. It broke away from the herd and became lost in the blurry sea of boulders that loomed in the half darkness of the storm. Possessing the agility of a red deer, it bolted from boulder to boulder and eventually crossed over into the adjacent ravine.

Like a good herdsman, Pappa decided to go after the animal. The herd would continue toward the top, the old ones having made the journey many times before. He instructed Petter to stay with the pack reindeer which was dragging the gierehtse that carried their possessions. The boy also had Puc to keep him company. Much of Puc's stiffness had worn off as the day progressed and he walked along beside Petter, limping but with a mind full of determination and a belly full of warm mush. He was enjoying the climb in spite of his recent ambush.

The day was growing darker, as much from the snow-storm as from the night creeping into the ravine, already full of ominous shadows. The howling of the wolves was muted and distorted from the wind, making it difficult to pinpoint their position. The sound echoed from side to side in a stereo effect. They could be anywhere and everywhere. Even their yellow-green eyes were wasted in the obscurity of the shad-owy light.

Pappa followed in the same direction that the young reindeer had taken. He had to climb over huge boulders and inch his way into the next ravine. The cold hardness of the forsaken land set him to shuddering. He was lost in the darkness. He thought he saw his reindeer and headed in that direction, only to discover that what he saw was a scraggly bush next to a boulder. Another time, he followed the movement of a dark form to his left. Certain that it was his reindeer, he moved closer and closer. The animal either recognized him or was frightened witless, for it did not move. Pappa had no choice but to continue on up the ravine.

The wolves became quiet in their quest. They found their prey. It was a matter of time before they would over-take another victim in their battle for survival. Their actions were governed by their hunger and they were about to assuage that craving.

Petter became uneasy because Pappa had been gone too long. He was glad he had Puc beside him, but he was worried about Pappa even though Pappa had his gun and knife. Petter would have heard the echoing sound of the gun above the noise of the wind. To ease his own anxiety he talked endlessly to the dog and hoped that Pappa would return soon. The herd had settled down and was moving at a steady pace toward the ridge. Still there was an eerie silence that frightened Petter.

Suddenly Puc stopped. His head went up and his mouth opened to savor the scent that wafted through the air. He cocked his head back and forth, trying to understand what he was hearing, piecing together the sounds the wind blew asunder with wisps of the distasteful scent. The hackles on the back of his neck went up, making him look much taller and twice as ferocious. His innate intelligence drew him into the blackness. Without a backward glance, he followed his senses, leaving the boy alone with the herd. Puc must find Pappa.

The reindeer had formed a narrow column as they went up the ravine, twelve to fifteen abreast. Many of the calves tagged along with the cows. Others mixed with the older bulls. The pack reindeer, Petter, and Puc brought up the rear. The sound that Puc heard came from the left of the column, from the direction Pappa had taken. He followed the loathsome scent that had already intersected Pappa's trail.

Another ravine paralleled the main pathway. It was into this ravine that the frightened reindeer had fled. Pappa had followed it and was trying to keep up with it, all the while talking to soothe it. At least it was heading up instead of down or across like the wild deer and moose do when they are on the move. Pappa knew the two ravines would meet and become one as they reached the ridge. He was no longer concerned for the reindeer. He knew that he was in a precarious position himself—alone, in the dark, and without protection.

Confident that the young reindeer would follow the ravine to the top where it would join the rest of the herd, Pappa became more concerned about the wolf pack. They had been silent too long. That was not a good sign. He had his gun, but he used it only when all else failed. The Samis prided themselves on living a peaceful existence and relying on the gifts of nature to eke out a simple life. There were times when man had to take the upper hand when dealing with the forces of nature. He used the gun last night, and he would use it tonight if the pack forced his hand. He believed that all beings were a part of the natural order of things and that, being a part of that natural order, he must respect the role of the pack—unless it posed a threat to his livelihood as it had last night. He was prepared to offer resistance.

Pappa had his knife at his side, and he could use it as skillfully as anyone. He could skin a wolf as easily as he could peel the delicate skin from a tiny blueberry. That thought was foremost in his mind as he saw a crouched form loom into the path in front of him. His heart almost stopped as another silent figure brushed against his leg. His heart felt as if it would burst. He must be surrounded by the entire wolf pack. True to his training from early childhood, Pappa controlled his urge to gasp, to run, to show any outward sign of fear.

The warm glow of adrenaline gave him new strength. The pairs of yellow-green eyes hung in the air like fiery opals, suspended in space. For a fleeting moment he took his eyes off the motionless form in front of him, certain that it was a wolf. He looked down at the form that had brushed against him, fearful that he would see another wolf. There was no mistaking the gray animal walking beside him. Instead of a gray wolf it was a gray dog—Puc.

Only the freezing temperature kept the tears from streaming down his face. Grown men do not cry, even when they experience the deep life-saving loyalty of a dog—at least that is what they would have people believe. Puc was no match for the wolf, especially in his weakened condition. But the wolf did not know that, and Puc did not even consider it. Puc felt the same allegiance to the man and boy as the gray dogs had felt for their masters far back in time when wolfdog decided to befriend man while wolf went the way of the wild.

Pappa kept walking deliberately toward the wolf, gun raised, calling its bluff. Puc stayed at Pappa's side, growling menacingly. The wolf, a clever animal in its own right, sensed the imminent danger of the situation. It had learned to fear man—especially when man had a dog and a gun. Like an untrained hunting dog that switches trails in the hopes of finding an easier prey, the wolf disappeared behind a boulder, and the rest of the pack followed. Pappa reached down and patted Puc, gently scratching the dog behind its ears. Puc responded by arching his back and leaning against the man's legs. A slight flicker of the dog's tail was the only acknowledgment that Pappa received, but that was worth all the salmon in the Tana River.

Petter was in no danger. He could be alone for a little while. It was good for him to have the responsibility of the herd. It would make a man out of him. There was no immediate danger from the wolf pack. The wolves were in this ravine and would not cross over where the boy and herd were. The young fugitive reindeer would be almost to the ridge where the first of the herd would be emerging from the ravine by this time. The frightened animal would be all right once it joined the others.

Pappa caught himself rationalizing, trying to justify having the dog at his side. He knew Puc belonged to Petter. But, for this moment, in the void separating reality and fantasy, the man walked in peace on top of the world with his gray dog at his side.

Atop the Ridge

he wind was gnashing at the mouth of the ravine, waiting to snatch the unwary traveler, making even the strong stagger against its push and pull. The top of the ridge had been relieved of everything but bare rock through centuries of being pummeled by the unrelenting force of the wind. Not even the snow was able to accumulate to any extent except in late winter when the wind rested for short periods. Then as much as a meter at a time would pile up, creating icy cascades of water to gush down the ravine when the early spring thaw began.

The reindeer emerged onto the brief plateau, pausing only long enough to savor their ascent into the forest. With a toss of their antlered heads and the clicketyclack of their hooves on the barren rock, they dared the wind to force them back down the ravine. Instead, they headed for the other side where they knew they would find the life-sustaining lichen and the protection of the trees, the forest that was their winter home just above the village.

In small groups of twos and threes, fives and sixes, the reindeer cavorted up, across, and down. The young runaway reindeer, racing up the adjoining ravine, gave a loud snort and a triumphant kick of its rear legs as it rejoined its family. Petter had a difficult time holding the pack reindeer back when it sensed it was home. He led it as slowly as he could along the slippery rock, the tent poles echoing stiletto refusals with each step the reindeer took.

Once in the safety of the trees, Petter loosened the harness that held the gierehtse to the animal, letting the pack drop to the ground. The animal, glad to be rid of its bothersome burden, gave a defiant kick and joined its cohorts in the sanctity of the forest.

The tired boy lay down on the abandoned pack, curled up in the warmth of the reindeer skin, and waited for the arrival of Puc and Pappa. He would have gone on home, but he preferred to wait because he wanted to arrive in the village with his gray dog beside him for all his friends to see and envy.

Pappa was enjoying the blissful solitude—just him and the dog—with no worries. The long hike up the mountain was over, and he would soon be back in the village. The herd was already in the forest above the village, safe for the winter, of that he was certain. Petter was probably waiting in the forest so that they could go back to the village together. He knew Petter would want the villagers to see him with his new dog. The gray dog had something else on its mind, however.

Puc was no longer limping. The tear in the flesh on his flank was barely noticeable. The stiffness of the early morning was more from being flung down on the rocky ground than it was from being bitten and torn. The fight for survival exceeds expectations in this arctic area where only the fittest do survive. Puc would be a better dog for having wrestled and survived.

When Pappa and Puc emerged from the ravine, Puc kept his nose to the ground, unusual for a gray dog, but he had to catch the scent before the wind picked it up and added it to the ever changing potpourri of fragrances. He zigzagged across the ridge, the strong wind seemingly pulling him by his gray fur. The wind let go of his coat on the other side and Puc delved, headfirst, into the forest. His head came up as he tasted the tantalizing scent of the forest.

Instead of following the well-worn path behind the reindeer, Puc paralleled the ridge, heading away from the village. He moved deliberately and silently. The spongy floor of the forest was a healing relief to his feet after the long trek up the rocky ravine.

Pappa called to Puc when he reached the top of the ridge—but to no avail. The wind caught his voice and played catch with it, fumbling it to the winds below. He watched helplessly as Puc took off in the opposite direction. It was useless to try to call him back. He would just have to follow the dog and hope that the dog would not go too fast. Pappa was tired and wanted to go straight to the village and his house.

The scent of the moose was too strong for Puc to resist. The moose and its mate had been rudely displaced by the returning reindeer and were out searching for solitude. The moose was surprised when it sensed the gray dog on its trail. Puc followed the big animal across, down, and around in a big circle. The moose intercepted the trail of its mate and would have joined her except that the dog closed in and circled it just inside a small clearing. The cow stood in a clump of trees nearby and watched.

Puc tightened his circle around the bull. The bull, very much aware of his silent adversary, eyed him at first with idle curiosity. It stood still until the dog began a shrill, incessant barking. The moose, wanting to be rid of the interminable pest, became agitated. To further annoy the moose, the dog darted in and out, nipping at the big animal's hocks and flanks. The moose kicked defiantly, determined to get rid of the dog and the shrill barking that was as great a pain to its sensitive ears as the nipping was to its legs. Puc was keeping the moose at a stand just like his mother—Leidi—had taught him to do one morning at the camp when he was a very young puppy.

Pappa might just as well have stayed where he was instead of trying to follow because Puc had circled back very close to the path where they came up over the ridge. As Pappa followed, he lost track of Puc again. All of a sudden he heard the shrill, nonstop barking, the signal that gray dogs give their masters when they have a moose at a stand.

Pappa had heard it many times when the hunters were out with their dogs. He had watched the hunters when their dogs began their peculiar barking. He knew, then, what he had to do. He had to do it for Puc more than for himself. With his gun ready, Pappa crept silently toward the sound.

Meanwhile, Petter fell asleep while waiting for Pappa to join him. He was not prepared for what happened next. He was awakened abruptly from the warmth of his fur covered pallet on the gierehtse. The strange sound, the shrill, excited barking of a dog, startled him. He had never heard a dog bark like that before. There was no doubt in his mind that it was Puc, but he did not know why Puc was barking like that. The barking continued. Petter shook his head to clear his thoughts and made an instant decision to run toward the direction of the barking. He wanted desperately to find Pappa and Puc.

Just as he jumped to his feet, a shot rang out and the barking stopped—there was silence. His heart sank and he feared for the worse. He remembered the night that Pappa shot the wolf. Maybe the pack had followed Pappa over the ridge. Pappa would do anything to save the herd. Maybe he did not know the herd was safe in the forest. Even the young renegade reindeer was back and settled in. Petter must run and tell Pappa not to shoot anymore.

Petter ran as fast as he could through the forest toward the sound. Just as he thought his lungs would burst from the cold air rushing through his lungs, he heard growling and muffled half barks. He stopped behind a big tree and peered into the small clearing in front of him. There in the middle of the clearing was sprawled the biggest moose he had ever seen. The shovels on its monstrous head lay at an angle across half the clearing, forming a gate which kept the boy from entering its sanctum. The spread of the dead moose's antlers must have been more than two meters.

Petter could barely see Pappa on the other side beyond the moose's head. When Petter spotted him, he had one foot resting on the flank of the moose and was holding the barrel of his gun in one hand with the stock resting on the ground. Pappa looked like he was in shock and was still staring in disbelief at what had happened.

Petter could hear the dog but could not see him. The moose's head wobbled as Petter took hold of the big shovels to find a way around the giant mound of flesh. Peering through the branches of the antlers, Petter caught sight of the dog. Puc was up on top of the moose, digging with his feet and tearing at the hairy animal with his teeth.

Since Pappa was not a hunter, Petter had never been around scenes such as he was facing. He did not know that it was customary for a hunter to let the dog pull at the moose like Puc was doing. This was the hunter's way of rewarding the dog, letting him lay claim on his trophy. Otherwise, the dog may not want to track and bring a moose to stand again.

Pappa did not know this either. He was just so flabbergasted at what had happened that he was too exhausted to do anything else but watch. Pappa and Petter, oblivious to one another's presence, watched Puc until he tired of his fruitless activity and jumped off his mountain to lie down in satisfied triumph at Pappa's feet.

Pappa sat down beside the panting dog, praising him for bringing the moose to a stand and telling him how proud he was to have such a good dog.

The boy read the sincerity in his

father's tone. Pappa called Puc his "egen grahund." Petter
was stunned. A feeling he had not experienced before
moved all the way up into his throat. Puc was Petter's dog,
but Petter just heard Pappa call Puc his very own gray dog.
Petter was angry, hurt, jealous. He was not a hunter and he
did not want to become a hunter, but Puc was his dog not
Pappa's. Pappa was not being fair.

Petter, blinded by tears, slipped away from behind the
huge antlers that separated him from the two most important
things in his young life and disappeared into the forest.
Pappa would never even know he had been there. If Puc
knew, he had not let on.

Petter did not stop at the gierehtse to wait for Pappa.
He made his way back to the village and the security of the
simple wooden house where he lived with his family. Shat-
tered were the visions of his triumphant return to the village
with his very own gray dog. It was getting so late that no
one was outside to see him anyway. Pappa may have taken
Petter's dog, but at least he would not be able to show off the
dog to the villagers when he came home.

Petter was greeted at the house by his mother and sister.
They questioned why he was alone and where Pappa was.
Petter explained that Pappa was getting the herd settled in
the forest and that he would be home in due time.

Petter politely refused his mother's offer of a bowl of
warm mush, saying he was not hungry. He curled up on a
reindeer rug and was sound asleep when Pappa came home
later that night, leading a pack reindeer that was pulling a
gierehtse loaded with fresh moose meat. A tired Puc trotted
along quietly behind him.

The Big Hunter

PAPPA SPENT THE NEXT FEW DAYS PRESERVING the moose meat for the impending cold spell. The families in the village had no refrigeration or freezers. Although they preserved some foods by salting them heavily or storing them in brine, the most common way to preserve moose meat was by a smoking process. The process dried it out, making it somewhat tough, but at least it kept the meat from spoiling.

When the family still lived in a tent, the tent had a smoke hole at the top where the poles met. It was a simple matter to hang the meat on stakes outside where the smoke from the fire inside the tent would drift across the slabs of meat on the outside—the fire, thus, serving a dual purpose. Now that the family lived in the village in a permanent house, Pappa built a smokehouse. It was more of a lean-to shed where he could keep a low, smoking fire going, filling the inside with dense smoke. The slabs of meat were hung from the rafters of the shed where they were smoked until well preserved. The slabs remained hanging there until needed, and the shed became a stabbur, or storage house, for the family's winter food supply. In this way, the meat was out of reach of wolves, bears, stray dogs, or anything else that might enjoy a feast at the expense of the family.

Puc made himself at home under the house. He seemed to remember his puppyhood in these surroundings and adapted quickly to the routine of the household. He rested the first few days, seldom coming out from under the house except to eat the scraps that Petter threw out for him. After a while he began to follow Pappa around as Pappa took care of the herd and got ready for the winter.

One evening Pappa went to the town meeting which was held in the school building. Petter could just hear his father bragging to the other men about his very own gray dog, the wolf pack, and the big moose. Some of the other men at the meeting had lost reindeer to the wolf pack, too. They discussed ways to solve the wolf problem. All of them dreaded having to stay with their herds and wasting the wood on fires to keep the wolves away. The alternative was to hunt the wolves down and shoot them.

While Pappa went to the town meeting, his family stayed at home. They sat around the fire on throw rugs of reindeer furs until the warmth made them sleepy. They were all dozing, enjoying the comfort of home, when an abrupt thud hit the floor from underneath the house. It sounded like Puc was fighting with another animal. Petter wanted to get Pappa's gun and shoot whatever it was, but his mother said no. The growling, gnashing, and gnarling continued for what seemed like a long time.

When it finally stopped, a low rumble continued under the house. Petter and his sister rubbed a clean spot in the smoky window to peer out. They could just barely make out the limping form of one of the stray dogs of the village, headed down the path toward the edge of the village. When the stray was far enough away and out of sight, Petter went out and knelt by the house. He called softly, "Puc. Puc." Puc crawled out from under his domain and rubbed up against Petter. Puc had dealt with strays before, and he wanted no part of them. His usual bluff had not worked with this stray, but his quick nipping and sharp teeth did have an effect. The stray dog would not come under his house again. This was his house and he was going to protect it.

Petter's mother called him inside to go to bed. He would go to school tomorrow. He had missed many days of school because he was with Pappa and the herd. Pappa wanted him to learn the ways of the Sami. There would be plenty of time later to learn to read and write and do numbers.

His mother wanted more than the village school for Petter. She had gone to a village school and she wanted her children to have at least that much, but Petter was special. She talked with him about going to Kirkenes to secondary school and, maybe later, to a university to study. Petter often dreamed of leaving the village and going to a big university. He would study hard and become famous. He would not have to eat mush and sleep on reindeer skin rugs and live in a log house because he would have lots of money to buy the things he read about in his school books. When Pappa came home from the town meeting the family was asleep, dreaming of easier times.

After a good night's rest the family was up early and busy with chores. Petter rekindled the fire with a few sticks of wood and brought enough wood in to last his mother the day. They all ate their simple morning meal of mush, flat bread, and to celebrate the hunt, moose meat.

As soon as Pappa finished eating, he went to the clearing to check on the herd. He would like to have called to Puc to go with him, but the dog still seemed worn out from his bout with the wolf. Petter did not tell Pappa about Puc's fight with the stray dog under the house.

When Petter finished his chores, he told his mother that he was going to school. He left with an old reindeer skin rolled up and carried under his arm. He told her that he was taking the rug because it was too cold in school, and he needed it to keep warm. He called to Puc as he was leaving.

Instead of following the path toward the school where the happy noises of a playground intermingled with the songs of the birds and the barking of the stray dogs, Petter took the path toward the ridge. He shifted the rolled rug from one arm to the other as he walked—and Puc followed. Petter talked to Puc the entire time, telling the dog that he was Petter's very own gray dog—not Pappa's. When Petter was certain that he was far enough away from the village so that he would not meet any of his friends on their way to school or pass by where Pappa was tending the herd, he stopped.

Very carefully, Petter laid the rolled reindeer rug on a bed of spruce needles under a tree and unrolled it. Puc watched curiously. He wiggled with excitement when he saw the gun. Petter's hands shook as he picked up the large caliber rifle. "Finn!" he said to Puc. "Finn!"

Puc instinctively understood. He began sniffing the air and the ground around him. He trotted around the tree and widened the distance between himself and the boy. He held his head high, scenting for a sign that a moose had been in the area. In a very few minutes Puc found the scent he was after and took off at a trot. Petter followed awkwardly, toting the heavy gun.

They went farther and farther into the forest. It became harder and harder for the boy to keep up. Puc went up toward the ridge and back down. He went toward the clearing where the herd was and Petter's heart sank. That is where Pappa is! Just before he reached the herd, Puc zig-zagged and went farther down the side of the mountain. Much to Petter's relief the dog headed for the same general area where Pappa shot the other moose.

Just as Petter felt that his short legs could not take one more step, Puc circled a large clump of trees. A dark form was barely visible through the trees. Petter watched in utter amazement as Puc worked. Without a sound, Puc maneu-vered the moose into full view. It was a cow, as ugly an animal as ever lived. Cows have no antlers and are smaller than the bulls. Nature has not graced them with a great amount of beauty. Puc had no trouble getting her to move through the trees. But then he began that interminable high-pitched barking. Petter was so afraid that Puc would be killed by the cow's kicking and charging as the dog darted in to nip at her. The spectacle continued for a long time until it suddenly dawned on Petter that this was what hunting was all about—now he was supposed to shoot the moose.

Petter's arms were trembling so hard that he could scarcely pick up the heavy rifle, let alone fire it. He managed to balance the stock of the gun on his shoulder by leaning up against a tree for support. He knew he was supposed to close one eye and look at the moose and squeeze the trigger. Before he could do that he had to put the gun down and take off his heavy mittens so that he could find the trigger and then go through the balancing process again to get the gun back on his shoulder. He closed first one eye and then the other. The moose was becoming agitated with the dog and beginning to move. The boy knew he had better pull the trigger or the moose would be gone. He could barely reach the trigger with his short, stubby fingers, but he pulled with all his might.

"Nei, Petter, nei!" Pappa came running from the clearing where the herd was grazing, calling frantically to his son. The moose took off in the opposite direction. It may have been startled by Pappa's screaming. It may have been agitated beyond the point of endurance by the long time the dog had been circling it. It may have gotten a whiff of the boy as the wind shifted. At any rate, it was out of sight with Puc in hot pursuit.

Pappa had not taken any courses in child psychology. No one had told him how to talk with his boy. He knew that Petter was having problems dealing with his feelings. He knew that Petter was struggling with feelings of jealousy because Puc had bonded with Pappa. He wanted to do the things Pappa did, but he was still a child.

Pappa did what any other Sami pappa would do. He
gently took the gun from the boy's trembling hands and
began talking to him. He explained that he shouted at him
because he was afraid Puc was in the way and might get
hurt. He explained that the rifle was too powerful for Petter
to try to shoot. And he explained—with a great sigh of
relief—that the gun misfired because there was no shell in its
chamber.

Pappa took the gun and told Petter that they had better
hurry if they were going to be in position to shoot the moose
when Puc brought it to stand again. It was several hours
before they caught up with the dog but, being the natural
hunter that he was, Puc got the cow into position for Pappa
to shoot. Pappa took aim at the spot behind the shoulders of
the quivering animal and squeezed the trigger.

They let Puc lay claim on the slain animal as he had its
mate. This time, however, when Puc was tired of pulling
and digging at the moose, he went over and lay down beside
Petter, as though saying, "Vi er et fint lag, ikke sant!" or as
Petter was learning to say in English, "We make a fine team,
don't we!"

Pappa asked Petter to go get one of the reindeer to use as
a pack animal to drag the meat back to the village. Petter
ran off, glad for the opportunity to get away from the gory
mess. He did not mind leaving his best friend with his next
best friend. He would not be gone long.

When Petter came back with a reindeer, he helped
Pappa finish gutting the moose, and together they cut poles to
use as a gierehtse. They harnessed the gierehtse to the
reindeer and loaded it with the moose carcass. When the

work was finished, the hunting party headed for the village.

It was a big day for Petter as he and Puc wended their way along the village paths, followed by the reindeer pulling the gierehtse—and Pappa. There was no doubt in the minds of any of the villagers who saw them that the beautiful gray dog belonged to the boy with the big smile on his face.

Missing Child

THE SNOW WAS COMING DOWN LIKE IT DOES much of the time in the Arctic. Day had turned to night. Pappa prepared his family for the worst in case the ice giants of the North decided to play their usual havoc. Petter made sure that there was an ample supply of wood for the cooking fire. He piled it high near the front door and brought more than the customary pile inside. It was not unusual for the snow to drift higher than the windows of the house. It was fun for the children to burrow out the front door to the stabbur or to the woodpile. Pappa did not think it was much fun. He worried about the herd. Even though the wolves had never crossed the ridge, there was always a first time.

The family read well into the evening. Nordic people read much of the time during the long cold winters. There is not much else to do when they are confined to the house, especially in the evenings. Petter and his sister were enjoying the adventures of Lief Ericson and Erik the Red, favorites of many Scandinavian children. Their school teacher had assigned a chapter in their history books for them to read, and they were supposed to write a report about one of the explorers' adventures. Both children enjoyed school. Petter's sister especially enjoyed staying late to help the teacher get the room ready for the next day.

The house was quiet except for the occasional creaking sounds caused by the howling of the wind. The family could hear Puc under the house. He had chosen a spot as near Petter's bed as he could get. Once in a while when Puc was digging his bed a little deeper or rearranging it, he kicked a rock up against the underneath side of the floor. Sometimes Petter tapped on the floor to let Puc know he had gone to bed. When he tapped on the floor tonight as he crawled under the warm reindeer skin cover, Puc sneezed in response. Petter laughed and he could almost see the answering quiver of Puc's furry tail.

It was a heavy snow, although not as deep as Pappa thought it would be. There were no excuses to stay home from school today. The children ate their warm meal of mush, smoked meat, and reindeer milk and bundled up for the walk to school. They would have no problem getting there if they stayed on the paths. The trees sheltered the walkways and kept the snow from drifting over them. The paths were kept worn down by the rough playing of the children as they went to and from school. Many of them stayed out after school to play, and the paths were their playgrounds.

Puc smelled the meal cooking from above him. He could not understand why the family was up because it was pitch dark under the house. He crawled to his usual way out from under the house but it was closed. The snow had completely blocked him in. He heard the front door open and the children come out. He burrowed toward the sound and surprised them when his black muzzle and head suddenly appeared by the door. They laughed as Puc pulled himself onto the path that was already being packed down by the traffic of the busy household.

Puc's usual routine was to follow the children to school. When they were safely inside for the day, he trailed Pappa when Pappa went to check on the herd or gather wood. Sometimes Pappa worked at the mine. Puc was not encouraged to go that far from the house. Pappa was afraid someone would steal him.

On the days that Pappa worked at the mine and the children were in school, Puc had to find ways to pass the time. If he got a strong whiff of a moose, he followed it, often bringing it to a stand. He would bark and bark but Pappa never came to shoot the big animal. The moose would suddenly break away and disappear into the forest. Puc would tire of the game and amble back to the house. After checking to make sure that no edible scraps had been thrown out the door for him, he crawled back under the house for a long nap.

On this particular morning, after the children went into the school, Puc went back to the house. He had missed his morning meal, and he knew it would be eaten by another hungry animal if he did not find it first. Sure enough, his meal was waiting for him. Someone had poked the leftover mush and a bone through the snowy hole under the house. Puc gobbled the mush and took the bone to the nest he had slept in. He gnawed on it until he fell asleep in the warm darkness.

Puc usually managed to be at the school when the children came out, but today was different. He napped all day in the quiet of his den and did not realize afternoon had come until he heard the children laughing and playing. Petter called to him, and they had a fine time rolling and tumbling in the snow. Petter was hungry after a hard day of learning and decided to go inside.

The first thing his mother wanted to know was where his sister was. Petter shook his head. He had not seen her after school but, then, she probably stayed to help the teacher. The other kids called her yndling or "teacher's pet."

It was snowing again, harder than yesterday. Daylight was fading fast, and Petter's young sister still was not home.

When Pappa came in from the mine an hour later, he said he thought this would be the heaviest snow of the winter, and that more than likely they would be snowbound by morning. When he found out that his daughter had not come home from school, he ordered Petter to dress as warmly as he could and to bring his snowshoes. The two of them looked like furry animals as they emerged from the house wearing the awkward-looking snowshoes and carrying poles for balance.

Pappa whistled for Puc. The dog made his way out from under the house. He growled when he saw the two furry forms. Petter giggled and Puc looked embarrassed when he realized it was Petter and Pappa. Pappa was worried about the girl and in no mood to be amused. He knew what could happen if they did not find the child immediately. They set off in the direction of the school, Puc leaping behind them. "Finn!" Pappa almost screamed. "Finn!"

They made their way along slowly, calling the child's name. The only sound they heard in the darkness was the whistling of the wind, and even that was muted by the heavy falling snow. Puc sensed the seriousness of what they were doing. He knew they were not tracking moose because Pappa did not have his rifle. Besides, they did not track moose in the village along the path or in deep snow. They always waited until they were in the forest before Pappa said, "Finn!" Puc knew he was supposed to find something, but he did not know what. They made their way as far as the school. The building was dark and the doors were closed.

Pappa knew then what had happened. The girl must have stepped off the path into a drift. The path was already deep with new snow. "Finn!" Puc would make a leap, stop and scent—leap, stop, scent. He still was not sure what he was supposed to find, but whatever it was, if it had a scent, he would find it—even in the snow. Puc could find anything. He could even scent over water. He used that skill often when he was alone in the forest, wading in the streams. When he smelled a trout, he grabbed it and had a good, fresh dinner.

"Finn!" Pappa was beginning to panic. Petter felt guilty for not looking after his younger sister. He tried not to think about what it would be like if they could not find her. Pappa would blame him and so would his mother. They would not want him anymore. He would go away and not come home. He would find his way to Kirkenes where he could go to a secondary school. Pappa and his mother would be glad he was gone.

"Finn!" came Pappa's command. Puc was beginning to tire. The only way he could move was by leaping. Sometimes, if his leap took him off the path, he could not even get his head above the snow when he landed. One time the snow was so deep that he had to burrow back to the path where Petter and Pappa were walking along on top of the snow, wearing their snowshoes. They prodded the drifts with their poles as they felt their way along in the darkness, but Puc had to leap along the path or burrow through the drifts.

They were about halfway back to the house when they came to a turn in the path. One way led to the church and

the other way led home. A noisy stream followed the turn
in the path. It was a favorite place for the boys to play after
school. The rushing of the stream was barely audible tonight
because it, too, had burrowed under the snow. It was not yet
frozen by winter's latest rage. Puc was used to wading in the
stream. He welcomed the cold dip even now. He discovered that he could follow the stream without having to leap
in and out of the deep snow. He was enjoying the familiar
sights, sounds and smells, although they looked and sounded
quite different in the deep snow than they did at other times
of the year. He had walked this way many times with
Petter. They often walked along the rocky bank on their way
home from school, but the girl never did. She was told to
stay on the path because she might fall and hurt herself.

Puc could not understand why he kept getting the scent
of the girl and not Petter. She should not be here. Above
the thrashing sound of the stream muted by the snow Puc
heard Pappa's frantic, "Finn!" The girl. He had her scent.
She is here, lying in the snow. Puc began his shrill barking,
much like the signal that he gave when he had a moose at
stand. He did not move. He just stood there. Again he
barked.

Petter and Pappa made their way as quickly as they
could to the sound of the barking. The snow had drifted to
an unbelievably high level for that early in the winter. As
the stream made a bend around a clump of trees, it exposed
itself where the trees sheltered it from the snow. It was here
that Puc was standing guard over the still form of the girl.
She obviously misjudged the curve in the path and became
disoriented. Her calls for help could not be heard above the

gurgling of the stream and the howling of the wind. There
was no one out in the darkness to hear her anyway.

Pappa picked her up and laid her over his shoulder. He
had to leave one of his arms free so that he could use the pole
to get back on the path. The strange-looking group made its
way back to the house as quickly as was possible in the
storm. Puc stayed behind them on the path, afraid to let any
of them out of his sight.

When they reached the house, the snow was halfway up the door. A wall of snow fell into the room when
Petter pushed the door open. They burst inside and Pappa
laid the girl on the reindeer skin rug in front of the fire. It
was Petter's job to scoop the snow back out the door before it
melted. If that happened, the water from the snow would
freeze around the door and they would not be able to go in
or out. The house was not usually warm enough to melt the
snow by the door, but they would build a bigger fire tonight
to keep his little sister warm.

The mother knelt beside the still child. She quickly
replaced the frozen clothes with dry ones, gently massaging
the child's feet and hands and cooing to her. When the little
girl's eyes flickered with life, the mother pulled the child onto
her lap. As she cuddled her, she spooned tiny sips of warm
broth into her mouth. Everyone sighed with relief.

Pappa smiled to himself when he caught sight of
Petter out of the corner of his eye. Petter had filled a bowl
with the warm broth and slipped quietly out the door. He
found the hole that Puc had burrowed to reach his den
underneath the house. Puc extended his arm as far as he
could and set the bowl down. Puc nuzzled Petter's arm in

appreciation for the meal. After the grateful dog slurped up the rich broth, he fell asleep in his nest under the house below the boy's bed. If dogs dream, he very well dreamed about the time he fell into a snowdrift when he was a little puppy, and Leidi found him—much the same way he had found the little girl just a few hours ago.

Fire

THE LONG, HARD WINTER DRAGGED ON AND on. The snow accumulation was well above the windows. Snow tunnels led from the door to the endless stack of firewood and to the stabbur where the supplies of smoked meat, smoked fish, cheeses, and meal were dwindling. The family spent the long days inside the simple wooden house, reading and doing chores. It was a time to catch up on mending torn leggings, sewing new jumpers, and working on the stack of reindeer skins. The skins were turned into rugs, bed covers, and clothes.

Pappa checked on the herd everyday. He was still afraid the wolves would get so hungry that they would come over the ridge. Puc went with him on these short trips. Pappa had made a small pack out of a reindeer hide to put over Puc's back. It had side pouches to carry rations and a coffee thermos. Puc knew that when Pappa came out with the pack that they were going to check the herd. He stood quite still for Pappa while he secured the pack with leather strips. The strips kept the pack from sliding off when Puc had to leap in and out of snow drifts.

Pappa let Petter bring Puc into the house to romp for short periods each day. He did not want him to get used to the warmth of the house. Dogs belong outside. They had to be able to survive in the snow and ice, the wind and rain. Still, he wanted to repay Puc for saving his little daughter's life. He and Petter would never have found her without Puc's help.

Puc's den under the house was almost as warm as the house. It was completely sealed with packed snow except for the small opening by the door. Some heat from the house escaped through the warm floor boards and was captured under the house. In addition to having a cozy den, the dog was almost as well fed as the family. Pappa knew Petter was feeding Puc more than was necessary, but he did not say anything. He was so proud of the dog.

Puc's coat had grown very thick during the cold winter. It is typical for all the gray dogs of Norway to have a double coat. They have a dense woolly undercoat covered by a harsh outercoat of longer hair that lies flat and keeps the warmth in. Even the dog's ears are covered with a thick, black, velvety fur that feels much like a mouse coat. However, his beautiful coat would be little protection against the arctic wind if he did not have his comfortable den.

Most of the households in the village were the same. The people knew what had to be done to survive, and they prepared for it. The smoke curling from the stove pipe was a sign that all was well. Families helped each other. If one ran short of supplies, others were willing to help as long as the man of the house worked hard to provide for his family. All in all, winter was a sleepy time for the village.

Puc was in his den asleep. He was used to the sounds and scents of nighttime. Petter often heard him yip softly as he dreamed of chasing a moose or romping with the children. Petter usually just smiled in his half-sleep and drowsed back to dreams of his own. The sounds and scents were different tonight. The soft growl and bark coming from under the house tonight were different, too. Petter sat up in bed, shaking the sleep from his head, trying to understand what was happening.

Puc's growling had turned into a full bark, and he left the confines of his underground domain, bumping his back on the floor joists as he crawled out. In a matter of seconds, Petter could hear the familiar shrill song, usually reserved for keeping a moose at a stand. "Pappa! Pappa!" Petter knew something was wrong. Pappa had heard the barking, too. Within moments they were both bundled up in their furs and out the door to follow Puc and find out what was wrong.

They could see an orange glow in the sky in the direction of Puc's barking. They followed the path in silence, knowing only too well what they would find. It happens each winter.

Someone gets careless, puts too much wood on the fire, a fur gets too close, or a child learns a tough lesson. They hoped that the unfortunate people were able to get out of the burning structure in time.

When they reached the brightness, the house was

ablaze. The adults were frantically yelling that the baby was still in the house. The man tried to go back in, but he was driven back by the intense heat. The baby was a two-year-old boy. Petter often saw him with his mother when he passed the house on his way to school. The father was attempting to crawl back into the burning inferno. He stayed close to the floor, calling the child's name. Everyone watched in silence. Even Puc stopped barking.

Petter knew that there was nothing he and Pappa could do to save the house. It was like a tinderbox. One more outburst of flame and the roof would cave in. He hoped the man could get back out with the little boy. And then it happened!

Quick as a flash, Puc leaped over the man and disappeared into the dense smoke. Petter gasped. "Puc! Kom tilbake!" Puc disregarded Petter's command for him to come back. Pappa grabbed Petter's arm to keep him from going after his dog. The man whose house was burning could be seen backing out of the doorway, driven back by the smoke and heat. The man was still on his hands and knees when Puc reappeared, dragging a frightened, screaming child by the sleeve of its leather jumper. The father grabbed the baby and darted away from his burning house, seconds before the roof and walls caved in.

The crumbling structure sent forth a dazzling fireworks display equal in intensity to that in Muspelheim—an endless pit of fire. Puc ran to escape the falling sparks and burning fragments of wood that scattered as the frame went down. He began rolling and rolling and rolling in the snow, snorting and burying his head. Petter ran to his dog, fell on his

knees, and grabbed for him. Puc stopped the rolling and
looked up at his young master. Petter cried out in disbelief
when he saw Puc. All he could do was to utter in an almost
inaudible voice, "Puc."

Much of the dog's hair was singed off. His black ears
were oozing like half-cooked bacon. His tail—the one characteristic that distinguished him from the wolfdog—normally
carried in a tight curl over his back and well covered with
silver-white hair, was covered with singed stubble. The
profuse ruff which usually looked like a furry harness was as
mangy-looking as that of a hungry wolf in a summer's shed
of coat. The tears rolled down Petter's cheeks as he looked
up at Pappa for help.

Pappa was not large in stature. He wanted to pick the
dog up and carry him home, and he would have, but he
knew that it would hurt the dog more than making him
walk. He wanted to hang a medal around Puc's neck. He
wanted—he wanted to get Puc home and tend to his burns.

The neighbors in the nearest house to the one that lay
in ruin took the unfortunate family into their home. The
child was more frightened than hurt, although he, too,
suffered serious burns. Fortunately for the child, he was so
close to the floor that there was little smoke for him to
inhale. The wooden building burned quickly and there was
not much inside that would cause smoke. The parents and
neighbors would let everyone know the extent of the
toddler's burns tomorrow.

The villagers trudged back to the warmth of their beds,
the shock of a house burned to the ground still not registered
fully in their minds. Only after they see the blackened

embers in tomorrow's bright sun will the stark reality of
what happened register that which the stupor of sleep erased
from their minds last night. Many children will be paraded
past the rubble to receive a lesson in reality on what happens
when children play with fire.

Pappa gently heaped mittens full of snow all over Puc.
The cold softness of the snow helped draw out the heat from
the blistered skin. As the snow melted over Puc's hot body it
washed away the singed hair from the once beautiful gray
coat. When they reached their own house, Puc headed
under the house. Without a word Pappa opened the door
and called Puc into the house. Together, Pappa and Petter
applied a liberal coat of bear grease to the burned areas of
Puc's body, his nose, ears, tail, and the pads of his feet. They
left him on a pallet beside Petter's bed and, once again,
summoned the night.

Puc spent most of his time for the remainder of the
winter under the house to stay warm. Pappa continued to
apply grease to the burned areas and to clean the sores that
became infected. It took weeks for the blisters to break, scab
over, and heal. It took even longer for the hair to grow back
and for the coat to become lustrous again. His ears lost their
velvety feel, and as they healed they developed a build-up of
scar tissue; however, Puc's keen sense of hearing was not
affected.

The child's hair was singed and he screamed in the
middle of the night for weeks. He suffered more from
trauma than from burns. He made a full recovery and, for
months, whenever Petter and Puc passed by his house, he
would run after them and pat Puc on the head.

The burned house was rebuilt on the same site with the
coming of the spring thaw. It was not the first house to be
consumed by fire nor will it be the last. A people who live
as closely by the laws of Nature as the Sami people in the
village understand that Nature often reclaims what was
taken from her in the first place and only the fittest survive.

Word soon spread over that part of Norway about the
brave gray dog in the village. Hunters heard it at the trading
posts. They took the story to their families who spread it
from town to town. The dog became a hero in his own
right, a legend to the people in Storskog.

It did not take long for the story to travel by word-of-
mouth to the larger towns as soon as the deep snow had
given in to the warmth and new life of spring. Relatives
visited relatives. Friends visited friends, in stores, in homes,
and in hospitals. Everyone was talking about the brave dog
that had rescued a little girl from a snowdrift and saved a
little boy from a fire in the Sami village.

In a nursing home near a hospital in Kirkenes sat a
man who was once a hunter but would hunt no more. As a
result of a hunting accident, he had lost his legs. He listened
intently to the story as a visiting doctor told it to one of the
nurses. The nurse turned to the man in the wheelchair and,
in a teasing manner, asked, "Tror du at en av dine hunder
kan ha gjort det, Osh!" ("Do you think one of your gray
dogs could have done that, Osh!")

The Thief

MANY RIVERS ETCH THE SURFACE OF NORWAY in brief, exaggerated swiftness. Their icy blue waters seem to lace the rocky terrain together to keep it from falling into one of the cavernous fjords. The rivers disappear sometimes, hiding among the trees, and then say, "Gotcha!" when they rush out and tumble over jagged rocks in a foamy display of white water. More often than not their banks are smooth layers of granite, like long banquet tables, waiting for someone to add floral centerpieces and have a party. Their sun-warmed banks are a shocking contrast to their chilled waters.

The rivers are innkeepers for trout and salmon, thus, becoming the hosts for feasting bear and other carnivora that are quick-handed enough to partake of the fare. Though the fish glide through the mirrored water in a syncopated ballet, they are not as easily plucked as the blueberries that are in abundance on a grassy hillside. Perhaps that is why, in the golden era of Asgaard, clever Loki changed himself into a trout to escape punishment from the gods for his wicked deeds. Loki, ironically, was plucked from his icy refuge by, of all things, a gray dog, friend of the gods. One might even surmise that the trout's tail was thus shaped into a vee when the gray dog pulled it from the waters and its tail has remained that shape through the centuries.

On the smooth, layered rock of the particular river that ran in close proximity to the Sami village, another gray dog had just finished his meal of fresh trout, one he had snatched from the river's cool depths. Puc had come to the river with Petter and two friends to catch trout for their families. Few people fished the river. The fish were running in abundance. The boys had little difficulty catching all they could handle. They had their stringers loaded with fish and were tying them to a jagged rock in a shallow pool where the fish would remain, refrigerated in the icy water, until the boys became tired of playing and headed back to the village.

Summer is a perfect season. Even though it is short and cool, the days are long and filled with new life. Many varieties of colorful flowers grow in every crevice, every pocket of soil, creating a palette of color that more than likely Edvard Munch, Norway's internationally known expressive painter, could not have resisted. Blueberries, raspberries, and cloudberries adorn the hillsides in Christmas tree splendor, another of Nature's gifts for the enterprising people of the North, who make the berries into jams for the winter. Even as the boys enjoyed their fishing expedition in the Hurtig River, the reflection of the snowcapped mountains looming overhead were a constant reminder to them that winter was waiting to happen.

The river, at this point in its brief meander, was like a huge reflecting pool. Its tabletop banks were warm from the summer sun. It was a good place to run, climb, and play the rough games in which boys the age of Petter and his friends like to indulge. They fished until they got bored with fishing. They played until they got bored with playing. They rested on the warm rock table until they became restless. There was nothing else to do but to go swimming, even though their parents had forbidden it.

White water boiled in a frenzy farther down river, but there was none here. The boys were familiar with the pool and could not resist the temptation. They shed their scant clothing, scattering it on the flat rock in the process. They enjoyed another of Nature's gifts, swimming as freely as the fish that darted helter-skelter to hide in rocky shadows when the three boys took to the water.

Puc took a nap in the shade of the forest after his dinner of trout. He, too, was ready for a swim. He joined the boys in a water fight, paddling back and forth from one to another, until it was not fun any-more. He climbed up the slippery rocks and pulled himself out onto a shelflike ledge. There he shook himself until he looked as dry as he was when he jumped in. The boys went on playing while Puc looked elsewhere for adventure.

He sniffed the clothes that he found strewn about the rock. The scent on the tunics was that of the boys, made even more pungent by the warm rays of the afternoon sun. In fact, he savored the scent of Petter's tunic and leggings so much that he picked them up in his mouth. Looking around for a likely place to put them, he decided they would make a good bed. The sun was too warm for a dog with a coat as heavy as Puc's, so he dragged Petter's clothes into the forest where he had taken his nap earlier in the day.

Not yet ready for another nap, Puc went back to the river to check on the boys. As he passed the scattered clothes, the aroma again caught his attention. He sniffed them over carefully, not finding anything that belonged to Petter. Oh, well. That will not make any difference. He picked up some clothes that belonged to one of the other boys and dragged the pieces to his new pad in the forest. With the additional clothes as padding, he had a bed fit for a king.

Still not ready for a nap, Puc went back to the river to check on the boys. As he passed what was left of the clothes, he stopped to sniff, circled the clothes several times, and plopped down on top of them, watching the boys in the water. He scratched the clothes around periodically to get more comfortable. The pallet still did not feel right so he decided to take the remaining clothes to the forest where he had stashed the other pieces. All that remained on the rock were three pairs of moccasins.

The boys eventually got tired of playing in the water. Actually they had worked up an appetite and were hungry. They decided they had better head for home before their parents started to worry. They each had a full stringer of

beautiful, fat trout to take back to the village where they
would be praised for providing food for their families. And
they had fun. Petter was the first to climb out onto the
welcome warmth of the rocky ledge. The heat felt so good to
his shriveled feet that he was reluctant to put on his moccasins. He decided to put on his tunic and leggings first, then
his moccasins.

"Vare klaer er borte! Noen har tatt vare klaer!" he
shouted. In English this means, "Our clothes are gone!
Someone took our clothes!" The other boys splashed out of
the river and came running to Petter. They thought he was
teasing. They hurriedly slipped on their moccasins and ran
up and down the riverbank looking for their clothes. There
was not a trace of a tunic or a pair of leggings anywhere.
They knew Petter was not teasing.

Girls! The girls must have taken their clothes. All
three of the boys had sisters. The brothers and sisters liked to
play tricks on each other. The sisters were good friends and
often thought up things to do to make life miserable for their
brothers. The girls were probably watching them right now
and giggling over their practical joke.

The boys looked for something to wrap around their
nude bodies. There was nothing, not even any leaves. The
only trees near the river were scrubby old spruce and the
needles would scratch. They would have to walk back
through the forest, hoping to find that the girls had hidden
their clothes behind a tree. If they could not find their
clothes, they would just have to make a run for their houses
as soon as they came to the village.

With that plan in mind, the boys untied their stringers of fish from the rock and headed into the forest. The fish were heavy and the boys were tired from their day's work—actually from their day's play. They certainly did not appreciate someone's idea of a prank.

Petter and his friends looked behind each tree as they made their way toward the village but to no avail. When they got to the edge of the forest, approaching the village, they knew what they had to do. They each tied their stringers of fish around their waists. As small waisted as they were, the stringers reached around three times. The fish flopped sporadically, making the boys wobble to maintain their balance when they walked.

Never had the birds of the forest seen such strange-looking animals. They screeched and flew to higher branches. Never had the stray dogs of the village smelled such fishy boys. They followed closely behind. Never had the village cats seen fish walking down the paths of the village. They moved in behind the dogs for a closer look.

Never had the children of the village seen such a sight. They laughed and pointed and sang, "Fish til salgs! Fish for sale!" The boys could not run. The trout were too heavy. The best they could do was struggle toward their houses. The parade passed the other boys' houses first. Those two boys disappeared inside and several of the dogs and cats dropped out of the parade in anticipation of being thrown scraps when the fish were gutted.

The diehards followed Petter. His house was last. As he approached his house, the commotion wakened Puc who was having such a good nap in his new bed under the house that he did not get up. The clothes that he had dragged home from the river bank were so soft and comfortable. He would go out and play with Petter later. Right now he must nap on his new bed.

When Petter confronted his sister and accused her and her friends of stealing their clothes from the river bank, she laughed, saying, "Not even a dog would want your smelly old clothes!" The way Petter heard the taunt from his sister was, "Ikke en gang en hund ville ha dine illeluktende klaer!" The way Puc heard it was, "That will teach Loki to turn himself into a fish!" He yawned and was sound asleep on top of a pallet of smelly old clothes before Petter could unwrap the stringer of fish from around his waist.

The Intruder

THE UNCERTAINTY OF AUTUMN MAKES IT the time of year to bask in the sun or put on parkas and mittens or take a ride in the snowmobile or get soaked to the skin by a sudden rain shower. One thing was certain, however; winter was on the doorstep. Every drop of rain dampened the spirits of the villagers. They knew the icy drops would become snow and the snow would imprison them once more.

The dreariness of the weather did nothing to ease the sorrow in the wooden house in the village. Puc was gone. He occasionally went off to the forest and was gone for hours at a time, but he had never been gone for as long as two days.

Petter held back the tears each morning as he went to the edge of the forest and called and called. He put warm mush and a bone by the door of the house each morning before he went to school in the hopes that Puc would return. He raced home after school each day to see if the dog had come home. The food was always gone but there was no sign that Puc had eaten it.

Pappa missed the dog, too. He did not realize what a big help Puc was in herding the reindeer and keeping the stray dogs under check. Pappa was spending long hours at the mine. Maybe he should have spent more time with the dog. Hunting season would open soon but he did not stand much of a chance of filling the stabbur without a hunting dog to track the moose. Last winter he and Puc brought in enough moose to feed the family and to help less fortunate families who had run out of provisions before the spring thaws brought relief.

One of the lessons of life that Petter was learning was to take happiness when it was offered and to search down new paths when it was taken away. The lesson was more in keeping with life in the Arctic than the one Petter and his sister were struggling with for their homework. They were sitting at the table reading the chapter in their history book that the teacher had assigned. It was raining outside and the light hanging over the table caused weird shadows to flicker across the pages of their books. It was difficult enough for Petter to concentrate on something that had happened hundreds of years ago without imagining that one of the shadows looked just like a gray dog. He was just about to capture one of the shadows in his hands when he heard a familiar voice calling, "Puc! Puc!"

Petter ran to the door. Pappa was down on his knees, peering under the house. He was talking to Puc, telling him how glad he was to see him and coaxing him to come out. "Pappa!" Pappa jerked himself to his feet, looking embarrassed. He was wet from the pouring rain and exhausted from a day at the mine. He, like Petter, had chased an unlikely shadow in the hopes of capturing the missing dog.

Pappa came into the house and shed the dripping furs. He sat down at the same table with the children and ate his simple meal in silence. When it was time to turn out the light and go to bed, Pappa quietly told Petter that he was certain he saw Puc running up the path in front of him. They put food out for the dog as usual.

Pappa insisted that he saw Puc's tail end disappear as the dog crawled under the house. Petter lay on the floor by his bed and listened. He thought he heard the dog licking his feet the way dogs do when they finish eating, but Puc would have responded to his tapping on the floor by sneezing or with a soft yap to acknowledge Petter's presence. There was only silence.

The food they put out that night was gone

when Petter checked the next morning. Pappa had already checked before he went to the mine. Nevertheless, Petter set out another bowl on his way to school.

Pappa claimed he saw Puc on two other occasions. He said that Puc darted under the house, just like he did the first time. The phantom disappeared under the house and did not respond to Pappa's call.

Pappa came home from the mine earlier than usual the next afternoon because of an impending storm. He could hear the children coming home from school. They seemed to be louder and happier than usual. He turned onto the path leading to the house just in time to see a silver white tail disappear under the house. He rubbed his eyes to make sure he was not dreaming. This time he was positive it was Puc. He went into the house to get some mush to lure the dog out.

When Pappa came back out, he saw the reason for the children's excitement. In the midst of the group, tugging at their leggings and barking playfully, was Puc. Petter told Pappa that Puc was at school, waiting for the children to get out. He played with them all the way home.

Pappa put down the bowl of mush that he had brought out when he thought he had seen Puc go under the house. Puc ate it greedily as though he had not eaten for several days. Petter begged Pappa to let Puc come into the house for a little while. Pappa was as excited as Petter that the dog was back, yet he was confused. Although Pappa made an effort to sound disapproving, he agreed to let Puc come in for a little while.

That night, after Petter went to bed, he could hear the
familiar sounds of Puc's soft snoring. He could hear him
rearranging his nest under the floor near his own bed. In
fact, there seemed to be twice as much snoring and rearranging of his pallet. Content that his gray dog was home, Petter
slept soundly for the first time in days.

The next morning, Petter brought in the firewood for
his mother and then he set food out for Puc. Pappa watched
from the window inside the house when Petter and his sister
set off for school, accompanied by a jubilant Puc. Satisfied
that all was well, Pappa sat down to eat his morning meal.

Pappa was not going to the mine today. He had chores
to do around the house and then, with Puc's help, he was
going to check the herd. Puc should be back from escorting
the children to school shortly. Pappa put on his leather
leggings and parka in preparation for working outside in the
ever changing weather. Just as he opened the door, he saw
Puc slip out from under the house and head for the forest at a
fast pace. He whistled and called but Puc did not respond.
It was just twenty minutes ago that he had watched Puc go
off to school with the children. The dog could not possibly
have come back so soon.

About an hour later Puc returned to the house. He had
taken the children to school and made his rounds of the
neighboring houses to let the strays know he was back and
was still king. He sniffed around the door and under the
house. He came out from under the house and, holding his
head up in the air very much like he does when he is tracking a moose, he headed for the forest at a fast trot.

Pappa saw Puc and decided to follow him. He grabbed
his gun from the rack inside the house in case Puc brought a
moose to a stand. He started to walk as fast as he could in
the direction the dog had taken. He planned to check on the
herd anyway, and that was where Puc was headed. Pappa
could not keep up with the dog and soon lost sight of him.
He trudged on through the forest toward the herd. He could
see the reindeer up ahead. They were calmly grazing,
satisfying their constant hunger, oblivious to hard times
ahead. Pappa slowed his pace to catch his breath.

He sensed a flicker of movement in his peripheral line
of vision. He turned and caught sight of Puc. Puc's hackles
were raised as he walked toward a clump of trees. He
growled but his tail was wagging short, quick, little wags
and his neck was arched like he was looking down his nose
at something. Puc gave a funny little bark and his legs began
prancing up and down without really going anyplace. Pappa
stealthily moved in for a closer look, positive that it was not
a moose that Puc had at a stand. He had learned to read
Puc's signals for hunting, especially the rapid-fire, nonstop
barking and this definitely was not a moose.

Pappa caught his breath. For a moment he thought he
was seeing a reflection. It was almost like looking into the
mirrorlike water of a still pond and seeing his own face
staring back—only this was a likeness of Puc. Facing Puc
from inside the clump of trees was another gray dog. It was
not quite as tall, and it did not have the big masculine ruff
that Puc had. The silver gray color was the same. The silver
white tail that curled up over its back was the same, except
that the reflected image kept laying its tail to the side. The

two dogs seemed to be culminating the preliminary stages of a ritual that did not take Pappa long to figure out.

Puc turned and ran back toward the forest, constantly glancing back to see if the other dog was following. Pappa watched as the two disappeared. They never did see Pappa. Now Pappa understood the strange behavior of the past several days. Now he understood why the dog under the house did not respond to his call—it was the other dog—the reflection. Puc had found a mate—or the mate had found Puc. Obviously, the hunters still had not learned how to take care of their dogs and had let another one get away.

Pappa checked the herd by himself. Puc was too busy with other interests. Pappa had brought the reindeer back from their summer pastures early this year because something in his bones told him they were in for an extremely hard winter. Puc would be ready to help him when the time came.

The end of another day was marked by the joyous sound of the ringing of the school bell and the more joyous sound of the children. Pappa smiled to himself, wondering how he would explain the courtship of Puc and the newcomer to Petter.

The children were making their way in scattered groups along the village paths. They were pushing each other, shouting, laughing, throwing sticks and stones, all the things that children do because they are children—all but one. Petter was lagging behind the others, as forlorn as Pappa had ever seen him. He was looking this way and that way, searching behind every tree, every boulder, a look of utter desperation clouding his face. He expected Puc to be waiting for him when school was out, but the gray dog was no where to be seen.

Pappa stepped onto the path beside Petter. They walked to the house in silence. As they approached the door, Pappa gave a shrill whistle. The transformation in Petter's face was immediate when Puc slipped out from under the house and came charging toward them. He leaped toward Petter, knocking him to the ground. The two wrestled good-naturedly as Pappa watched and laughed. Petter freed himself of the dog's grip on his leggings and was about to get up when he yelled and pointed, "Pappa! Se!"

Pappa knew before he even turned to look what it was that Petter saw. The other gray dog was retreating under the house. He had seen it many times—the tail end of an intruder.

Jente

SNOW CAME EARLY AND WITH A FIERCENESS
that caught many people unprepared. Pappa had
provided for his family by filling the stabbur with smoked
moose meat and fish. Some of the blueberries had miracu-
lously turned into jam and the rest were dried into raisin-like
staples for eating and seasoning. Pappa had the best hunting
dog in the village which meant that his family had meat to
spare. He used smoked moose meat as tender to bargain for
grain at the supply post to make the mush and flat bread,
basic to all meals.

Pappa's work at the mine gave him extra money to buy
ammunition for hunting and fuel for the snowmobile. Life
in the village was tolerable and the family felt secure, not
dreading the winter as they had in the past.

The first snow came in the guise of a blizzard. It
covered any remaining vestige of plant life. Although it was
not deep enough to reach the windows, it did seal the under-

neath part of the house. Puc and his new companion, Jente, now had a warm, cozy den which most assuredly would stay cozy until late spring.

Puc burrowed a round opening just large enough to squeeze in and out. Petter spoiled both dogs by setting a bowl of mush and scraps inside their den. The two dogs had begun to roam at night and sleep during the day, a habit Petter did not like. He preferred to hear the muted snore and soft yips that Puc emitted during the night. In a way, he resented sharing Puc with Jente.

Puc emerged from the warmth of his den each morning to make the trip to school with the children. He usually met them in the afternoon, seeing them safely home through the drifts and snowball fights which he enjoyed as much as the children did. Everything worked into a relaxed, comfortable routine.

Jente had been with Puc for about seven weeks. Pappa noticed that she was fatter than when she first arrived. At first he attributed it to the extra food that Petter sneaked into their den. Then he remembered Puc's leave of absence two months ago and, when he did return to the family, his puppy-like antics after Jente moved into the den. Of course, he thought. That's it! She would probably have puppies in a few weeks.

Pappa recalled that morning two years ago when his family woke up to find a litter of puppies in the pulka. He was not in the least unhappy about the prospect of having more puppies. He has a snowmobile to show for the last litter. Visions of what this litter might bring began to pop into his mind.

Pappa reminisced about Leidi and the puppies and the day the hunters came to claim the dogs. The pleasant thoughts caused him to decide it would be a good idea to take Puc and Petter hunting. He was not much of a hunter himself but he wanted Petter to learn. If it were not for Puc, Pappa would never be able to track and shoot a moose by himself. Pappa went into the house to tell Petter to put on his parka for a hunt. Petter was not too thrilled, but Puc was excited when Petter called him out from under the house, and he saw Pappa with the gun.

Father, son, and dog climbed into the snowmobile and headed for the forest. Pappa stopped near a clearing, and Puc jumped out. He found a scent immediately and started trailing a moose.

Since Pappa had never been taught to hunt, he did not realize that the snow would be a problem. It was so deep in the forest that Puc was wearing himself out just leaping in and out of the deeply drifted banks in his efforts to track the moose. Pappa decided that going hunting was not a good idea after all, and he called Puc off the scent. They were returning home when they noticed another snowmobile just like their own parked beside their house. There were two men in it.

Petter's heart all but stopped when he saw the men. He called to Pappa to stop the snowmobile and let him out with Puc. He told Pappa that he would walk the rest of the way to the house. Instead of following the path, however, he headed toward the stream that lay almost hidden by snow several meters away. Puc followed him.

Pappa continued in the snowmobile the rest of the way to the house. He immediately recognized the hunters as Liv and Arne. He parked his snowmobile in its usual spot beside the stack of firewood where the pulka used to sit. He got out and walked up to Liv and Arne. The three men began the carnival-like routine of sign language as they greeted one another.

Jente was sitting between the two hunters, apparently happy to see them, ready and willing to go home with them. It was obvious that they were her owners. The men explained that she was their dog, and that she had become separated from them about eight weeks ago while they were in the forest hunting.

They were surprised, however, at how fat she was. Pappa explained, in a comical way, that she was going to have puppies. The men asked Pappa if he knew who the sire of the puppies was. Pappa pretended he did not know what the men were talking about. He also pretended that he did not know anything about another gray dog that ran away last year and had not been found.

Just then Petter came walking down the path toward the house. Along beside him walked a brown dog whose shaggy coat was dripping in mud. Pappa did a double take, but he did not say a word as Petter led the dog to the hole in the snow by the door and told the dog to go in. The dog gave a fierce shake and mud flew in all directions. With a flick of its tail, the dog went under the house.

The men nodded at Petter. They recognized him as the broken-hearted little boy who wanted to keep one of Leidi's puppies—in fact, the best puppy of the litter, the one that ran

away last year. Petter nodded to them and went over to
Pappa's snowmobile to watch the three men as they continued their pantomime.

Jente hopped out from between Liv and Arne when she
saw Petter. She wiggled all over. Then she ran into the hole
and disappeared under the house just as the brown dog had
done. Petter blocked the hole with some fire wood to keep

the dogs from coming back out.

Pappa was trying to tell the hunters to take Jente and leave. He wished he could tell them that he did not know who the sire of her expected litter was, and that he did not know anything about a missing gray elkhound with a small white star on its chest. Pappa was not one to lie, but if he could have spoken the Norwegian language that they understood, he would have sent them on their way with Jente.

While the men were gesturing to one another, Jente came bounding around from the back of the house. She was followed closely by the unattractive brown dog—except that the brown dog was not quite as brown as he was when he went under the house. The two dogs had burrowed out from under the house in the back. In so doing, Puc had cleaned and shaken much of the muddy water out of his coat. A good roll in the fresh clean snow caused his coat to return to its distinctive gray color. With his tail up and wagging, there was no mistaking him for anything but a gray dog of Norway, a most perfect one at that.

"Puc!" said Liv and Arne together. Puc cocked his head and looked quizzically at the strangers. The white star on his chest was even more noticeable when he looked at them with his head held high in his usual arrogant manner. He stared for a moment and then turned and trotted over to stand by Petter.

Arne and Liv grew excited. They knew that they had to act fast or Pappa would bargain them out of another snowmobile. Puc must be the sire of Jente's litter. There were no other gray dogs in the area unless one of the strays... Pappa, on the other hand, knew he had to act fast or the hunters would take both dogs and leave him without anything. Each was afraid of being outfoxed by the other.

Arne and Liv talked in hushed tones, which was not necessary, because Pappa could not understand their Norwegian anymore than they could understand his Sami dialect. Arne took a piece of paper and a pen from his pocket and began writing in Norwegian:

I, _____ , do certify on this the 15th day of November

that the gray elkhound known as Puc, from the Leidi x Grom litter, was bred
to my gray elkhound known by you as Jente on 3 September.
In return for the care given to Jente and the breeding to her by Puc,
I am now the sole owner of the gray elkhound known as Puc.
The signing of this agreement is witnessed by
Arne Christiansen and Liv Vole.

Arne handed the paper and pen to Pappa. Using the same sign language that Pappa used to bargain the hunters out of their snowmobile, Arne pointed to Jente and Liv with one hand and to Puc and Petter with the other hand. He then motioned for Pappa to write on the paper on the blank line. Pappa recognized some of the words on the paper. He understood the sign language better.

All three men wanted to get the bargaining over with before someone started pointing to someone else's snowmobile. Pappa signed his name to the paper. With smiles of relief, they all shook hands. Not to be outdone, Puc raised his paw to Petter as if to seal an already solid relationship.

The men called to Jente and lifted her gently into their snowmobile. They left by way of the same path that they had used when they left that other time in the snowmobile, pulling the pulka that held Osh, Leidi, and her puppies. They were just as relieved to be leaving this time as they had been before. At least they found their lost dog, and she was soon going to have a litter of puppies—and they still had their snowmobile!

Petter and Puc began playing. Now Puc was really his very own dog. Petter rubbed him down with snow. Pappa smiled to himself as he watched the brown-looking dog turn to his beautiful silver gray color. Maybe his son was growing up to be like his father after all. Not even Pappa would have thought to color the dog brown.

The Avalanche

THE SNOW WAS DEEPER THAN PAPPA EVER remembered. Paths through the village ceased to exist when the powdery white flakes reached the meter mark and were totally forgotten when the depth climbed unbelievably higher. School, the children's main link to the outside world, closed. Town meetings were called off because no one could find the town hall and no one wanted to talk about the dreary weather anyway. The lone church in the village was denied its once-a-week Sunday worshipers because the church, like the other buildings, was inaccessible under the deep snow.

Few people ventured out of their houses. They had everything they needed to survive within easy reach. The woodpiles were outside the doors; enough food for days was kept inside the house and enough for the entire winter was kept in the nearby stabbur. There was always a kettle of warm food sitting on the stove. Those daring individuals

who braved the outdoors were often easily disoriented
because familiar landmarks were obliterated under the deep
white camouflage. No one risked going out except in emergency cases which, for Pappa, was taking care of the herd.
He would lay down his life to care for his reindeer. The
other herdsmen depended on Pappa to know when to take
the herds to summer pastures, where to take them, and when
to bring them back to the forest near the village.

The reindeer were hungry. The herdsmen moved them
into the forest as close to the village as they could get. The
snow was not as deep in the forest and there was more
lichen—their mainstay—for them to eat. The reindeer dug
through the deep snow with their sharp hooves to get at the
lichen. There was nothing above the snow for them to eat
unless they tried to eat bark from the trees. It was not only
the reindeer that were hungry. All the animals were hungry,
including the wolves.

Pappa's worst fear became reality. For the first time he
could ever remember, the wolves came over the ridge. He
had a sickening feeling in the pit of his stomach when he
was awakened in the middle of the night by the first mournful howl. He hoped it was a lone wolf, one that had broken
away from the pack out of sheer desperation for a meal. His
heart sank when he heard a second, third, and echoing
howls signaling the arrival of the entire pack. He dressed in
his warmest furs, grabbed his gun and snowshoes, and went
to join the other men.

The men knew that they either had to fight the pack or
lose their herds. They worked in shifts, day and night,
patrolling the forest. They soon had a deep rut worn in the

snow, a race track that enclosed the reindeer in the forest. Smoky fires smoldered in strategic locations, partly to discourage the wolves, partly to keep the men warm.

Villagers who had dogs brought them along—even the strays were coaxed into service. The dogs provided companionship and alerted the men to the position of the wolves. Having their dogs with them gave the men a false sense of security because the dogs would be no real threat to the starving wolves.

Pappa spent most of every night traversing the forest in his snowmobile. Puc sat in the seat next to him, growling at anything that moved and bristling with hatred at the repulsive scent of the predators. When he figured he had accomplished what Pappa had in mind, he curled up on his reindeer skin rug and slept.

The night was as bright as the day; the beams from the full moon like icicles penetrating to the depths of the men's souls. A strange quiet fell over the forest as the moon slipped below the mountaintop. Pappa stopped near one of the dwindling fires to add a green log and to stretch his legs. The green log would create a denser smoke screen as well as cause the fire to burn more slowly. Puc jumped out of the snowmobile for a look around.

When Pappa was satisfied that the fire would not go out, he got back in his vehicle and started another lap around the restless herds. He called out to the sentries posted farther inside the tree cover as he passed. Puc loped along behind.

The snowmobile was moving as slowly as it would go without stalling. There was no hurry. Pappa could hear the howls getting closer and closer. He could see the yellow-

green eyes, like distant fireflies, dancing in the dark. The
wolves became quiet as Pappa approached. His angry shouts
sent them slinking for cover, and the yellow-green lights
blinked momentarily. The wolves were apprehensive toward the man and cautious of his dog because it carried the
human scent they loathed. The wolves, however, intended
to remain until they fed on the reindeer or until spring
thaw—whichever came first.

Pappa continued his endless laps around the herds. Up
ahead, a young stag reindeer had wandered away from its
herd in search of better grazing. It was close to the outer
perimeter of the protected area. Pappa saw it as he passed
and sent Puc to move it back with the rest of the herd. Puc
began to nip at the stag, running first on one side of it and
then the other, in an effort to move it farther into the forest
with the rest of its herd. The stubborn stag was determined
to have its fill before it returned to the others and was reluctant to cooperate with Puc.

Without warning, there came from the shadows a huge
wolf, which, in one leap, lunged for the stag's throat. Puc
wheeled. He was so incensed by the repugnant smell of
wolf that his only thought was to kill. His leap intercepted
the wolf and they both fell to the ground. The startled stag
bolted into the darkness of the trees.

Unless they are at the point of starvation, wolves are
afraid of humans and will slink away in fear. They seem to
hold a fearful respect for the herdsmen's dogs as well. This
hungry wolf knew, however, that it had to rid itself of the
pesky dog before it could give chase to the reindeer. Puc, on
the other hand, had not forgotten his deadly encounter with

the wolves in the hunting camp. Neither had he forgotten
how he walked along beside Pappa on the way home from
summer pastures, keeping the wolf pack at bay. The hatred
festering inside him gave rise to the belief that he could face
up to the entire pack of wolves without consequence. And
he tried.

Pappa heard the growling and yipping as dog and wolf
slashed at one another, each waiting for an opportunity to
grab the other's throat. The wolf lunged, getting a mouthful
of the thick hair around Puc's neck. Puc jerked free, wincing
as the skin tore from his body. He sprang for the wolf's
head, sinking his teeth into the loathsome animal's neck
behind its ear. The wolf reeled in pain, trying madly to wipe
the dog off by rolling over on him. It was difficult to discern
wolf from dog as their blood intermingled and soaked their
gray coats.

Pappa backed the snowmobile up where he could hear
the fracas, but he could not see a thing in the darkness of the
trees. He reached for his gun which was on the floor of the
snowmobile. If he shot toward the sound, he might kill the
wolf—or Puc. Instead, he shot into the air. The fighting
ceased. The only sound was the shouting of the herdsman
whose herd was in that area of the forest. Pappa called for
Puc, but there was no answer.

Pappa was afraid to leave the safety of the perimeter
path. He would have no difficulty walking on the snow in
the inner area because it was well packed from the reindeer,
but it was dark. He heard the bloodcurdling howl of a
hungry wolf, a sign that the wolf was ready to do whatever
it had to do for a meal. Green eyes stared at him from

within the forest as well as from the other side of the perimeter path of the snowmobile. The smell of fresh blood had excited the pack beyond control. Out of fear, Pappa shot once more into the air. The green eyes disappeared and the shouting of the herdsman came again, closer this time. Pappa shouted back, telling him to come faster. And then there was a terrifying silence.

Faintly at first, almost like the tinkling of a wind chime, it started. Pappa stood still, chills causing his skin to creep. It came again, a little louder this time, but not much. The two men shouted to each other again, trying to establish their positions in relation to one another. There it was again, hauntingly beautiful, yet painfully pathetic. The sound was barely audible in the stillness of the night.

Pappa made his way back to the snowmobile. He felt around for the high-powered flashlight that he bought recently at the supply post. It was under Puc's reindeer skin rug. Pappa grabbed it, turned it on, and aimed its penetrating beam into the darkness. He called again for Puc. In answer, he heard the crystal clear sound of tinkling icicles. He trained the beam in the direction of the sound. The beam formed an aura of light, engulfing the still figure of a gray dog, head momentarily raised to the moon. After its faint plea for help, the head fell to its bloody pillow of snow and waited.

Pappa ran to Puc and picked him up gingerly. With difficulty, he carried the bloody dog to the snowmobile. He told the approaching herdsman to use his gun if the wolves came back. Pappa made it quite clear to the herdsman that he was taking Puc back to the village. On his way there and back, he would spread the alarm and ask for additional patrols.

Meanwhile, Petter awakened to the sound of gunfire.
He could not go back to sleep, knowing the danger facing
Pappa and the other men in the village as they protected the
herds. He was relieved when he heard the approaching
snowmobile, although it did seem to be coming awfully fast.
Then he heard Pappa calling his name, telling him to come
quickly!

Petter ran to the door and opened
it just in time to let Pappa in with
something wrapped in a reindeer
skin rug. Without asking, he knew
it was Puc. Petter put some
wood on the dying fire and
drew a bucket of water.
Together they cleaned the
ugly gash on Puc's neck
where the wolf had torn off
the skin and hair. They bound up the wounds on his legs to
stop the bleeding and held cold compresses on the gashes that
could not be bound. Eventually the bleeding stopped.

When Pappa was satisfied that there was nothing else
he could do for the dog, he left Petter in charge and hurried
out the door. The fluttering eyelids and an ever so faint
movement of his tail were vital signs that Puc would be all
right if he could survive the extreme loss of blood. Petter
would spend the rest of the night on the reindeer skin rug
with his dog in front of the meager fire, the two of them
sharing what little warmth their bodies emitted.

Pappa went from door to door, mustering all available
men, telling them to bring their guns. It was his intent to

drive the pack of wolves back over the ridge, killing them if necessary. The smell of blood—part dog, part wolf—had excited the hungry wolves to the point that they would attack and kill anything that moved.

Pappa led his recruits to the battle site in his snowmobile. The men, clad in the skins of reindeer from the very herds they hoped to save, and wearing snowshoes, looked much like an army of saints walking on frozen water. The hair-raising howling of the wolves became chorus-like until a gun shot, having the same effect as a conductor's baton, brought the aria to a close. In a matter of minutes, like an encore, another soloist took up the refrain.

Pappa knew that he must take drastic action before it was too late. While he was rounding up recruits, he was devising a plan. His plan was to drive the wolves to the ridge and force them to retreat down the two ravines. The ravines were the only way up or down the mountain from the ridge. He told the men to form two lines which would act as a funnel or chute into the ravines. On a command from Pappa, the herdsmen advanced through the forest, leaving their dogs behind to care for the herds. The angry shouts of the men silenced the wolves and caused them to retreat toward the ridge in front of the two lines.

Progress was slow and dawn was breaking when the wolf pack reluctantly stood at the top of the ravines. Pappa advanced toward the pack in his snowmobile. At his signal, every man fired his rifle into the air. The startled wolves leaped over the edge into the ravines. At the same moment, a roar like the thunder of Thor echoed on the other side of the mountain. The men watched in awe as the ensuing avalanche, triggered by their gunshots, struggled down the mountain, leaving a clean path behind. It was many years before the howl of a wolf was heard again.

The men were too exhausted to speak. They went to their houses in the village and lay down to rest. They fell into a peaceful sleep for the first time since the brutal winter issued its challenge of the survival of the fittest. The complacent reindeer, with a childlike trust in the lone herdsman and his dogs, went about the business of nibbling on the moss and lichen.

Petter did not hear Pappa come into the house. He was curled around Puc, both of them sound asleep on the floor, wrapped in the warmth of a reindeer skin rug. Pappa looked about. His family was secure in his simple wooden house. The reindeer were safe in the forest. There was ample food in the stabbur. But yet it was such a long, dreadful winter. Pappa finally gave in to the gnawing fatigue and fell into a deep sleep.

A Medal

THE HEAVENS REFLECTED THE DREARY WEATHER by hiding the sun for weeks at a time. Even though winter raged on, the villagers rejoiced in the departure of the wolves and the safety of the reindeer who were surviving on their meager fare, oblivious to the plight of their predators. Pappa was weary of his self-imposed duty to protect the herds from danger, but he maintained a schedule that the villagers could set their clocks by.

He traced the race track around the forest twice a day in an endless effort to keep one step ahead of the heartless ice-giants of the North country—and to revel in the fact that the wolves were gone. All that could be seen of him as he wound around and around was the tip of his parka. He missed the gray dog that usually accompanied him—Puc, who sometimes rode with him in the snowmobile, some-times trailed along behind to catch the scent of a moose.

Pappa blamed himself every time he looked at Puc. The

dog had lain in front of the fire for days before he could even be carried outside for exercise. He winced every time Pappa picked him up and stood him in the snow outside. Pappa made him take a few more steps each time until, slowly, Puc regained his strength.

When Puc was finally able to go in and out of the house by himself, Pappa thought it was time for him to stay outside. Petter dug a tunnel in the snow so that Puc could go under the house. The dog was reluctant to go back to his old den, but Petter gave him a firm command and Puc disappeared without so much as a flicker of his tail.

The snows stopped eventually, and the familiar paths reappeared throughout the village, a sure sign that spring could not be far behind. The hustle and bustle of daily activities resumed, including school, church, and the town meetings. The tale of how Puc attacked the wolf to save the stag was told over and over. Puc became a legend in the village where he was already a hero for braving the fire to save a child and for rescuing Petter's sister from the snow drift.

On his first day back to meet Petter and his sister after school, Puc was greeted with a screaming ovation from the children. They idolized him, and he enjoyed every minute of the patting, tugging on his tail, and fetching sticks, back packs, and books. His dark eyes always sought out Petter, even when he was playing tug-of-war with someone else.

Nature betrayed winter's trust and sent gushing streams of melting snow down the mountainside. New life sprang into the seeds that lay exposed when their protective wintry blanket dissipated. The early flowers, eager now to emerge, quickly wove a lacy collage of color. A new generation of fowl voiced songs of surprise at each new day. And as the reindeer calves began to arrive, Puc took it upon himself to check out each one, daring the strays of the village to come near.

Pappa was hesitant to drive the herd to summer pastures, but he knew the food in the forest near the village was depleted. Deep down inside himself, he was afraid of the wolves, unsure as to whether he was afraid for himself or for the herd. To compromise his dilemma, he sent the herd with another herdsman and remained in the village with his family. He worked regularly at the mine and passed the long evenings of spring and summer by supervising preparations for winter—a vicious cycle of life.

As the weather cooled, Pappa and Puc bagged several moose. Petter was reluctant to go hunting with them. He preferred to go to school and to read. The teacher had planted the notion in his head of going away to school when he finished the last grade at the village school. Pappa was upset when Petter told him about it. He had been upset when it seemed that Petter would never grow up and become a man. Now he was upset when it seemed that Petter had begun to grow up and dreamed of a life beyond the day-by-day fight for survival in the village.

Petter wrote stories that described Puc's antics. He pictured Puc as the hero that found his sister unconscious in the snow. He wrote about how Puc wakened him during the night to rescue the child from the burning house. He described the burns that Puc suffered and how his ears still carry scar tissue from the burns. He told how Puc attacked the wolf to keep it from killing one of Pappa's young stags. Each story he wrote was better than the previous one. Each story portrayed Puc as a greater hero.

Petter's stories reflected village life and the Sami people. The teacher knew that Petter wrote from his heart when he described the saga of his beloved gray dog. The teacher was so intrigued with Petter's writing that she sent his stories to a friend of hers who was head of the department of education at the training school in Kirkenes. The friend, without consulting Petter's teacher, submitted Petter's stories to the local newspaper. The stories appeared in the newspaper. The local people were so intrigued by the stories about the gray dog that they begged for more information about him.

One day Arne and Liv drove into the village in their jeep. It was the first time they had been up the other side of the mountain. They had to come that way because it was too early for snow and the snowmobile. They came all the way from Storskog by jeep.

It was the weekend, and Pappa's family was home. A curtain of smoke hung low over the village, carrying with it the suffocating smell of meat and fish curing for the winter. Pappa greeted Arne and Liv with uncertainty, wondering what they could possibly want this time. Maybe Jente had not had puppies after all, and they wanted to take Puc. Pappa had news for them. Puc was not leaving the village!

Petter knew sufficient Norwegian to translate what Arne and Liv were saying to Pappa who understood only his Sami dialect. The men assured Pappa that it was a friendly visit. They talked long and hard, trying to convince Pappa to come to Storskog with Petter and Puc to see Jente's litter of puppies. They pointed out to Pappa that it would be an opportunity for Petter to see the world. Other than taking the herds to summer pastures, it was true that Petter—or Pappa, for that matter—had never been away from the village. Petter could barely control his excitement at the possibility of going to a real town, one that his teacher had told him so much about. Pappa relented.

As Pappa reflected on the discussion after Arne and Liv rode away, he wondered why he had ever agreed to such an unheard of thing. The village was good enough for him and the rest of the Sami people. It was good enough for Petter. He would tell Arne and Liv those very words next Saturday when they came to take him and his son away from their people.

Pappa had not counted on the excitement the news would cause in the village. Villagers were congratulating him for his good fortune and telling him how proud he must be of his son. Before the day's end, Pappa was congratulating himself for having finagled Liv and Arne into asking him to go. Pappa fell victim to his own conceit.

Petter's mother and sister spent many hours during the next week getting two suits of clothes ready, a new jumper made for Pappa and Pappa's old jumper tucked in for Petter. The jumpers were worn over leggings and the outfits were completed with large, round, pillbox caps. The caps were red and trimmed in braid to match the jumpers.

On the appointed day, Pappa and Petter were resplendent in their red jumpers with the white braid trim—their Sami costumes that were worn for festivals and special occasions. And this was a special occasion—Petter's first trip to town. By the time Arne and Liv arrived on Saturday, Pappa and Petter were pacing up and down the path waiting.

The entire village turned out to see them off. Puc sensed the excitement and barked himself hoarse. Pappa got into the back seat with Liv and Petter sat in the front seat with Arne. A proud Puc sat between them. The trip down the mountain road in a jeep was a new adventure for Petter. He was more than a little bit overcome with car sickness, but he was all right once they reached the town at the bottom of the mountain.

They went first to Arne's house in Storskog to see Jente and her litter of puppies. Jente would not let Puc near her puppies. Puc did not understand the cool treatment he received after their weeks of courtship. He stayed close beside Petter and pretended he did not care. There was no denying that the beautiful puppies were his.

Arne and Liv seemed to be in a hurry and did not take time to let Pappa look around. They got everyone back in the jeep and drove to Kirkenes. There was a group of people standing in front of a building in the business part of town. When the jeep drove up and parked at the curb, a band started playing. Puc pointed his nose toward the sun and joined in with the music. Everyone laughed and clapped as he howled to the sound.

Pappa and Petter's red costumes provided a startling contrast to Puc's profuse silver gray coat. Petter's sister had sewn together a matching red collar for Puc with the same edging as the costumes. He seemed to know he was special as he walked between Petter and Pappa. Arne and Liv ushered the trio to the top of a flight of concrete steps that led to the door of the town hall.

It finally dawned on Pappa and Petter that they had been brought to Kirkenes for a special reason. Puc was being honored. During the short ceremony that followed, a man—the governor—told of all the brave things that Puc had done for the people in his village. He talked about finding the little girl who had become lost in the snowstorm. He told about saving the child from the fire. He relayed the story of how the men purged their village of wolves and how Puc saved the young reindeer. In conclusion, he awarded Puc the coveted Carnegie's heltefond—medal and diploma—for his heroic behavior and outstanding service to his country. The governor was especially proud because Puc was a gray dog, the national dog of Norway.

Once again there were tears in Pappa's eyes as the impact of what was happening sank in. Puc posed for pictures, proudly wearing the red velvet ribbon with the gold medal lying against his chest. Almost as a reflection of the gold medal itself was the white star on Puc's chest. It showed just below the medal.

The three celebrities were taken on a tour of

Kirkenes. The tour included visits to the hospital, nursing home, and school. Puc loved the attention he received from the children at the school they visited. He became known as the star because of the star on his chest that showed each time he posed for pictures.

Arne and Liv told Pappa that they had one more place to visit before they began their trip back to the village. They entered another nursing home, this one filled with people who had accepted it as their home away from home. The residents were excited to see the aloof gray dog enter their hallways. They had seen his picture in the newspaper, but they had no idea that he would visit them in their nursing home. Puc shook hands with everyone who extended their hands and sat with his paw extended for those who were too unaware to understand his gesture. Others sat and gaped at the bright red Sami costumes worn by Pappa and Petter.

The visiting group passed through what appeared to be a dining hall of the nursing home. A long window at the end of the room was open and the lace curtain was floating gently in the warm afternoon breeze. The curtain brushed the face of the man who sat beside the window in his wheelchair. Arne and Liv led Pappa and Petter over to the window. They spoke to the man, but the man did not respond. Petter, who was learning to use Puc's disarming charm to hide his own shy demeanor, knelt down and whispered into Puc's ear.

As though through hours of patient practice, but in reality, a mere quirk of chance, Puc responded. He raised his head like he was searching for the moon. From deep within, there came a beautiful, clear, tinkling sound. The man in the wheelchair turned slowly toward the dog. His dull eyes lit up as he looked at the most beautiful gray dog he had ever seen. He struggled with a memory that would not clear itself in his mind, but lingered while he stared at the dog.

Puc stood in front of the broken figure of a man and stared back at him, waiting for the man to speak. As the dog's gaze and that of the man met, the elusive memory came forward. In an almost inaudible whisper, the man exclaimed, "Puc!" A slight flicker of the dog's tail was the only outward indication that somewhere, sometime, he and the man had met before.

EPILOGUE

OSH HAD FALLEN INTO A DEEP DEPRESSION
after his legs were amputated. Although there was little else
wrong with him, he knew his days of hunting were over.
His wife and son were unable to cope with his mental state
of mind. They had no choice but to make arrangements for
him to remain in the convalescent care center.

On the day his son told him of Leidi's death and that
Puc had run away, Osh withdrew from reality. His friends
visited him occasionally, but he did not respond. When they
located Puc in the Sami village, they began to plot a way to
bring the dog to Osh's nursing home.

Arne and Liv were torn between taking Puc away from
his young master whose heart had already been broken once
or withholding the information from Osh. They were
overjoyed when Jente and Puc mated. They hoped that
Jente would have a puppy so much like Puc that Osh would
respond.

Arne and Liv were overjoyed when Osh recognized
Puc. As a result of that one small glimmer of hope, they
organized the first known therapy dog club in Norway.
They used the gray elkhound because of its innate intelli-
gence and stability, and because it is the national dog of
Norway.

The road to recovery is as long and rugged as the jeep
ride up the mountain to the hunting camp where a weath-

ered old sign reads KRAEVIES BIENJE. Somewhere
behind the locked door of Osh's mind lay the memories of
moose hunts, Leidi, friends, and family. His family and
friends have hopes that the gray dog—one of Jente's litter—
that visits Osh once a week holds the key to that locked door.

A tattered newspaper clipping show-
ing a picture of a gray dog receiving an award on
the steps of City Hall hangs on the wall in Osh's
room. Underneath the picture, someone has
scrawled the word PUC. No one knows
who wrote it there. The locked door
opens momentarily and then closes.
Perhaps one day it will open
for one of Puc's sons
and remain open.

APPENDIX

Story setting

    Sami village near Storskog and Kirkenes in arctic
        Norway

Story characters

    Arne, Liv, and Osh - Norwegian hunters from
        Storskog

    Ola - son of Osh

    Pappa and Petter - father and son who live in a Sami
        village northeast of Storskog

    Leidi and Puc - gray dogs, a dam and her puppy

Proper names

    Pappa - Papa

    Petter - Peter

    Puc - Puck

    Leidi - Lady

    Jente - Girl

Cultural groups

    Sami - Samelat; indigenous people of Scandinavia
        and Russia; small in stature; pl. Samis,
        Samelats

    Lapps - a Ural-Altaic people inhabiting Lapland; also
        known as Sami or Samelats; formerly no-
        madic hunters and gatherers

Towns and regions

Alta - area in northern Norway where prehistoric rock drawings were discovered

Kirkenes - a major town in the arctic area of Norway

Lapland - an area extending across northern Norway, Sweden, Finland, and the Kola Peninsula of Russia; mainly inside the Arctic Circle

Storskog - a small place in the arctic region of Norway, east of Kirkenes

Norwegian translations

"Leidi fikk Grom's valper i dag. Vi drar i morgen for a finne henne." Leidi had Grom's litter today. We'll go tomorrow to find her.

KRAEVIES BIENJE - in Sami dialect (FOUND: GRAY DOG)

"Kom nå, Puc. La oss gå hjem!" Come on, Puc. Let's go home!

"Finn," commanded Osh. "Find," commanded Osh.

TUSEN TAKK A thousand thanks

"Nei, Pappa!" cried Petter. "Det er ikke en ulv!" "No, Pappa!" cried Petter. "It's not a wolf!"

"Se, Pappa!" Look, Pappa!

Min egen gråhund My very own gray dog

"Vi er et fint lag, ikke sant?" We make a fine team, don't we?

Puc! Kom tilbake! Puc! Come back!

Tror du at en av dine hunder kan ha gjort det?

Do you think one of your dogs could have done
that?
"Våre klaer er borte! Noen har tatt våre klaer!"
Our clothes are gone! Someone took our
clothes!
Fisk til salgs! Fish for sale!
"Ikke en gang en hund ville ha dine illeluktende
klaer!" Not even a dog would want your
smelly clothes!

GLOSSARY

Norwegian vocabulary

Asgaard - home of the lesser gods in Norse mythology

Carnegie's heltefond - the Norwegian hero foundation that awards a medal and diploma to dogs for heroic behavior, such as rescuing people or children from fires and drowning

Dyne - a featherbed or comforter filled with eiderdown

Elg - elk; a slightly smaller variation of the North American moose

Finn - v. find

Gierehtse - travois; pony dray; a crude drag made of poles that are stretched over with reindeer skin; harnessed to a work animal and used to carry possessions

Gravind - Wolf Night, the night, according to legend, that Norway was purged of wolves

Hurtig River - a swift river

Jente - a girl; the fictitious dog in the story

Julenissen - Santa Claus; Jul is Christmas, nisse is goblin/puck

Krone - the unit of currency for Norway; pl. kroner

Loki - a troublesome god in Norse mythology

Muspelheim - the home of fire in Norse mythology

Norsk Kennel Klub - the governing organization for the preservation of the stud book for the registration of dogs in Norway

Pappa - similar to papa; daddy

Primus - a spirit stove or petrol fire; a portable stove
used by campers

Pulka - a large wooden sled with a single runner;
usually pulled by reindeer

Stabbur - storehouse where staples are stored as
provisions for winter

Yndling - teacher's pet

General vocabulary

Brush - a bushy tail; a tail heavy with hair

Dam - the female parent

Double coat - having a weather resistant outer coat
that is protective against brush and brambles
and an undercoat of softer hair for warmth
and waterproofing

Eiderdown - the down of the Eider, a large northern
sea duck

Elkhounds - a group of spitz dogs native to
Scandinavia, i. e., gray elkhound, black
elkhound, white elkhound, buhund, and
jamthund

Flank - the side of the body between the last rib and
the hip

Gait - the speed and manner in which an animal
moves

Game - wild birds or animals that are hunted

Get - a collective noun denoting either the entire
representation or a sample of the progeny of a
given sire or dam

Gun-shy - when a dog is afraid of the sight or sound
of a gun

Hackles - hair on the neck and back that bristles or
raises involuntarily in fright or anger

Herdsman - the caretaker of a herd of domesticated
animals

Ice giants - the destructive giants in Norse mythology

Lichen - reindeer moss, reindeer lichen, or arctic
moss; a gray, erect, tufted, branched lichen
found on the ground in the arctic, forming
much of the food for reindeer

Litter - the collective group of young born of one
whelping

Muzzle - the foreface or head in front of the eyes

Pack - several wolves that run together and live
together

Pads - tough, shock-absorbing projections on the
bottoms of the feet

Pedigree - a written record of a dog's descent for three
or more generations

Prick ears - carried erect and usually pointed at the
tips

Purebred - a dog whose sire and dam are of the same
breed, each being of unmixed descent since
the origin of the breed

Reindeer - deer of the genus Rangifer in Scandinavia;
often domesticated and used in Lapland for
pulling sleds and as a source of food

Ruff - thick longer hair growth around the neck

Saddle - hair forming a black marking over the back

like a saddle

Scent - odor left on the trail by an animal—ground
         scent—or wafting in the air—air-borne scent

Sire - the male parent

Stud dog - a male dog used for breeding purposes

Trail - to hunt by following ground scent

Whelp - to give birth; a puppy or young dog; in
whelp - to be pregnant

Wind - to catch the scent of game

BIBLIOGRAPHY

Dreyer, Grondahl. History of Norway. Tangen Grafisk
    Senter A/S: Drammen, Norway, 1992.
Nilsen, Evald, trans. Steward Clark. Svalbard Arctic
    Norway. Aune Forlag As: Trondheim, Norway, 1990.
Ross, Nina P. Of Gods and Dogs, Norse Mythology.
    Towery Publishing Co.: Memphis,Tennessee, 1994.
Ross, Nina P. The Norwegian Elkhound. Doral Publishing
    Co.: Wilsonville, Oregon, 1995.